ANGELL AT 100

ANGELL AT 100

A CENTURY OF COMPASSIONATE CARE

FOR ANIMALS AND THEIR FAMILIES AT

ANGELL ANIMAL MEDICAL CENTER

by KAREN CAMPBELL

Published by LAMPREY & LEE
an imprint of Bibliomotion, Inc.

First published in 2015 by Lamprey & Lee
an imprint of Bibliomotion, Inc.
39 Harvard Street
Brookline, MA 02445
Tel: 617-934-2427
www.bibliomotion.com

Printed in the United States of America

PHOTO CREDITS
Page 16, Angell Animal Medical Center building, 2015, credit Topher Cox
Page 86, Charlie receiving his chemotherapy treatments, credit Stacey Escalante
Page 102, Carter Luke, credit Topher Cox
Page 105, The bustling lobby of Angell Animal Medical Center today, credit Topher Cox
Page 106, Dr. Lisa Moses, credit P. Carey Reid
Page 127, Dr. Douglas Brum, credit P. Carey Reid
Page 133, Siggy manning the phone, credit Jeanne David-Lee

All other photos that appear in this book were provided courtesy of the MSPCA–Angell.

ISBN: 978-1-942108-04-7
CIP data applied for

To a century of generous donors—those individuals, companies, and foundations—who have contributed so much to make Angell Animal Medical Center the world-class hospital it is today. And to a century of Angell staff members, who have given so many animals the precious gift of their expertise and loving attention.

Contents

Foreword

The MSPCA–Angell is an animal welfare organization that was founded in 1868 and is dedicated to making the world a better place for animals. Our history reflects our values. It was in our forty-seventh year, 1915, that significant change occurred in our thinking about what animal welfare really means. Animals in Massachusetts were facing a crisis: a shortage of veterinary care. Very deliberately, we took steps to address the problem. We built the Animal Hospital, and we dedicated it to our founder, George Angell.

That bold action was a statement that animal health and animal welfare are inextricably linked.

As we enter the one hundredth anniversary of that decision, I can't help but reflect on how that has made such a significant difference in real animals' lives. Animals face a lot of challenges in the world today. The MSPCA–Angell has many ways to help them with those challenges. Angell's doctors, nurses, technicians, interns, and residents have played a critical role in serving animals in need. Our medical team at Angell serves not only owned animals and their families, but also our cruelty investigators, our shelters, and our legislative efforts. The programs within our organization mesh. Angell treats, saves, rescues, diagnoses, and helps in a million ways to aid and inform the efforts of our non-medical wing—the Animal Protection Division. Our programs are inextricably linked.

One of the best examples of this is a dog named Stella. Stella was a five-month-old Lab mix, good natured, shy, and not completely house-broken. One night after she'd had an accident in the house, her owner decided to have some friends "get rid of her." But in the middle of the violent attack she suffered at their hands, she was rescued. She was brought to Angell alive, but with fourteen stab wounds. She needed the best veterinary treatment to survive, and she got it. Our law enforcement officers were notified, and the case went to court. Her case made headlines, and the laws were strengthened to make animal cruelty a more serious crime. And after her recovery, Stella got a new home.

The MSPCA–Angell recognizes that the fate of animals within our society is dependent upon the willingness of human beings to acknowledge the significance of their fellow creatures and to accept responsibility for their well-being. We are committed to programs and activities that create an enlightened and compassionate citizenry that is actively concerned with the protection of animals. We are all in this together. Inextricably linked.

Personally, my link to Angell began in the late 1970s. I was home in Wisconsin with my son, an infant who had some kind of visual problem. An ophthalmologist said that in order to diagnose the problem, a special test with some new technology was needed, but there were only three places in the country that had this technology: a hospital in New York, a hospital in Los Angeles, and a place in Boston called "Angell." He smiled and noted that the Boston hospital was for animals. Must be a special place, I thought . . .

Fast-forward to my first day with the MSPCA in 1985, when I was hired to oversee some of the Society's animal welfare programs. Chief of Staff Dr. Gus Thornton called me and told me that there was a piece of specialized ophthalmology equipment that needed calibrating, but he wanted it to be done using an animal already under anesthesia. He didn't want to take the risk of anesthetizing an animal just for the calibration. He wanted to find the safest and most humane way to achieve the end result.

Just before I moved to Massachusetts, I had adopted a new puppy, and it was time for her to be spayed. Great timing. I volunteered my young Lab, Chelsea, and during her surgery, she "helped" calibrate the machine. And that was the same machine that had helped diagnose my son Caleb's visual condition. Inextricable links and synchronicity.

A few years later, I met a young Critical Care veterinarian at Angell during a moment of sheer pandemonium. I had heard good things about her, but we hadn't been introduced yet. I was overseeing a cruelty case involving some cats that had ended up in the hospital. The cats weren't healthy, and they were all stressed and not very socialized. During a medical exam, one of the cats escaped and was loose in an exam room. It is not an easy task to capture a stressed and unsocialized cat. She was literally climbing the walls and cabinets, looking for a place to hide or escape. She knocked all kinds of things from the shelves—medicines, bandages, bottles, and equipment all flying across the room. It was chaos. There were two of us in the room: me and our new Critical Care doctor. I was about to ask her to leave the room, but she was calm and attending to the situation, and she safely and humanely captured the cat. Didn't need me at all. I was quite impressed. I've come to recognize that Emergency/Critical Care doctors are always focused like that in the midst of chaos. And they make good leaders. That doctor's name was Ann Marie Manning (now Greenleaf), and a few years later, she became Angell's Chief of Staff.

Angell is now one hundred years young. From the early years, animals and the MSPCA have been fortunate to have great people working for our cause. There is optimism in the house. The next one hundred years will be even better.

CARTER LUKE
President and CEO
MSPCA–Angell

The first Angell hospital

Introduction

Then and Now

It was a cold day in the winter of 1915 when the MSPCA first opened the doors of Angell Memorial Animal Hospital to the public. The brick and limestone building at 180 Longwood Avenue, in the middle of Boston's rapidly developing medical area, was staffed by five veterinarians. Horses were the hospital's primary intended patients in the early years, and the building opened onto a large courtyard with stalls and tie rings designed to accommodate equine patients. However, it wouldn't have been unheard of to see a society matron with her toy poodle sitting in the spare, crowded waiting room next to a young boy with his prize goat.

Fast-forward one hundred years, and the scene at the MSPCA–Angell's spacious state-of-the-art facility on South Huntington Avenue in Boston's Jamaica Plain neighborhood is very different. The bright and airy facility houses the two complementary facets of the independent, nonprofit organization—humane services and health care—all under one roof. The flagship hospital is now called Angell Animal Medical Center to better reflect the organization's comprehensive services.

The hospital's expansive entryway opens to a spacious lobby. Instead of seating the owner of a frightened, high-strung cat waiting for medical attention next to an owner with a boisterous one-hundred-pound dog, Angell provides separate waiting areas for patients according to species. Pets come in for everything from a nail trim to brain surgery, and owners often chat amiably with one another, sharing stories and comparing experiences. As staff members stroll through the lobby, they're apt to offer a greeting, a kind word, and a pat on the head for any nearby dog. Despite the occasional chorus of yips and meows, the tone during the day is generally calm. However, as in any big urban hospital, the energy ramps up with emergency situations, particularly during evenings and weekends. Angell is the largest veterinary facility in New England for 24-7 emergency care.

While the hospital works hard to maintain efficiency, there is concerted effort to generate an air of warmth and welcome. In fact, for nearly ten years, one pet owner visited daily—without his cat—just to sit and read the paper. And for a few weeks, one canine patient couldn't seem to get enough of the place. A boisterous neighborhood Husky who somehow managed to get out of his yard with great frequency bounded over to Angell, pranced through the electronic doors, and went straight to the pharmacy counter for the dog treats he knew were kept there.

There's a comfortable, familial feel among the staff, with frequent intern and alumni events, like a coffee and bagel repast for Friday morning rounds. Last year, the hospital started a staff vegetable garden. Staff members frequently bring their pets to work, and it's not unusual to find a Terrier contentedly gnawing on a chew toy on a blanket by an administrator's desk or a petite Pomeranian snuggly nestled on a warm lap while its owner works at the computer or runs a meeting. Photos and flashes of humor abound on exam room and office walls.

However, the dedication to providing expert animal care is anything but casual. "The vibe is that we do really great things here," says longtime staffer Mary Grace, Angell's Director of Hospital Operations. "Even when it's crazy and hectic, it's team-oriented, and there's a sense of pride and commitment."

The first veterinary hospital affiliated with a humane society, Angell maintains a world-renowned staff of roughly 80 veterinarians and 165 medical support workers. The hospital provides direct hands-on care for over 60,000 patients a year, including abused and homeless animals as well as animals with owners who need financial assistance to provide proper medical attention. Angell's call center, which has the buzz of a big city newsroom, often serves as the hospital's front line for worried pet owners, offering callers advice and facilitating connections with any of Angell's 17 specialty services.

The hospital's primary services range from wellness visits and follow-ups to cutting-edge emergency care, and amenities include a range of offerings for pets and their owners, from medical boarding options and a unique Client Care Coordinators program to financial aid and grief counseling.

Angell's waiting room in the early days

The Angell Animal Medical Center building in 2015

Angell offers emergency and critical care medicine around the clock, with specialty care ranging from acupuncture and behavior modification to oncology and neurosurgery, all under one roof. The hospital is the go-to facility in New England for complicated medical needs, facilitating collaborative treatment plans established among the hospital's specialists. Angell also provides 24-7 emergency service and specialty care at the MSPCA–Angell West in Waltham.

The mission of Angell Animal Medical Center is essentially the same now as it was one hundred years ago: "To provide the best possible medical and surgical care to animals, and to advance the practice of veterinary medicine to an ever-higher standard."

An Enlightened Partnership

Known internationally for its world-class veterinary care, Angell Animal Medical Center works in close partnership with the humane services side of the MSPCA–Angell. A national and international leader in animal welfare, the MSPCA–Angell's services include animal protection and

Farm animal and horse rescue center Nevins Farm, Methuen, MA

adoption, advocacy, humane education, and law enforcement. The organization's animal care and adoption centers take in as many as one thousand animals per month during the busy summer season. They provide vital services such as adoptions, behavior training, humane-education programs, and spay/neuter programs.

MSPCA law enforcement officers investigate cruelty complaints and inspect facilities and events involving animals to make sure they are being treated humanely. Often called to testify in court, they work with police and social-service agencies in animal-related cases. Officers are also committed to outreach and education, frequently speaking to school and community groups about animal care and protection. Advocacy staff members lobby for better animal-protection laws nationally and statewide. In addition, advocacy programs help support pets in housing and wildlife initiatives. The Spay/Neuter Assistance Program (SNAP) and Angell's Shalit-Glazer Clinic help facilitate responsible spaying and neutering for homeless animals and for pets from low-income households.

One of the MSPCA's most esteemed programs is Nevins Farm. Originally designed to care for retired police horses and other working animals, it is now the only open-admissions farm animal and horse rescue center in New England. Set on fifty-five acres of rolling pasture in Methuen, Massachusetts, Nevins Farm provides a haven for horses as well as an ever-changing assortment of pigs, ducks, sheep, geese, cows, goats, and more. Programs include rehabilitation and adoption of all kinds of farm animals, equine-rescue services, humane-education workshops, and summer camps for children. And adjacent to the farm for over eight decades is bucolic Hillside Acre Animal Cemetery, which provides a tranquil setting for the burial of more than eighteen thousand animal companions. The MSPCA-run cemetery offers a range of bereavement support and guidance for those saying good-bye to a beloved pet.

Throughout the MSPCA–Angell system, the emphasis is not just on the highest standards of individualized medical care, but also on personal attention and compassion—for animals, as well as for the people whose lives they have immeasurably enriched—a philosophy that was forged almost a century and a half ago from the fire of indignation and the heat of compassion, sparked by a Massachusetts lawyer and humanitarian named George Thorndike Angell. And while the organization of the twenty-first century is immeasurably more extensive and sophisticated than its initial incarnation, the philosophical heart behind its mission statement remains the same: "To protect animals, relieve their suffering, advance their health and welfare, prevent cruelty, and work for a just and compassionate society."

PART ONE

FROM PROTECTING TO HEALING, 1915–1976

I am sometimes asked "Why do you spend so much of your time and money talking about kindness to animals when there is so much cruelty to men?" I answer: "I am working at the roots."

GEORGE THORNDIKE ANGELL

George Thorndike Angell, first President of the Massachusetts Society for the Prevention of Cruelty to Animals, 1868–1909

CHAPTER 1

George Thorndike Angell: "Working at the Roots"

GEORGE THORNDIKE ANGELL (1823–1909) was born in Southbridge, Massachusetts. The son of a schoolteacher and a Baptist minister, young George was a bright, studious boy with a love of animals. He spent much of his boyhood on New England farms, and from an early age, he was known for speaking up if he heard of animals being mistreated.

Early in George's childhood, his father died, leaving the family penniless. As George's mother struggled to make their meager ends meet, he often ended up shuffling between a series of relatives, taking on odd jobs as a teenager. Yet he still managed to excel at school. He was accepted at Dartmouth College, where, according to one account, "his pronounced opinions, his sterling character, and his intelligence marked him as a leader." After graduation, he taught in the Boston public schools and attended Harvard Law School.

After passing the bar, Angell became not only a successful attorney but also a renowned philanthropist and humanitarian, known for his integrity and social commitment. An activist with a keen sense of justice, he worked for child welfare and penal reform, and he was a staunch abolitionist, partnering with antislavery advocate Samuel E. Sewall for fourteen years.

However, the issue closest to Angell's heart was the welfare of animals, and he became one of America's foremost pioneers in championing their protection and humane treatment. At that time, the intrinsic worth of animals remained a rarely embraced concept. Animals were still considered as property, primarily valuable only inasmuch as they were useful. As such, they could be treated in any way an owner chose, without interference. In the mid-1800s, conditions were especially bad for city workhorses, who were often overworked, underfed, and driven to the point of exhaustion, as their raw flesh chafed under heavy collars. Their lifespan was usually less than four years.

In 1864, two years before the formation of the first humane society in America, Angell decided to draw up his last will and testament, including these compelling words: "It has long been my opinion that there is much wrong in the treatment of domestic animals . . . and it is my earnest wish to do something towards awakening public sentiment on this subject." In the document, he stated his desire to donate a considerable portion of his estate toward "circulating in schools, Sunday schools and elsewhere, information calculated to prevent cruelty to Animals." He noted that he was determined to "plead for the wronged and oppressed, whether they walked on two legs or four."

Angell then became a leader in the movement's push for educating children, believing that humanity's kindness to all creatures could ultimately lead to a more kind and just culture overall. "Every humane publication, every lecture, every step in doing or teaching kindness is a step to prevent crime. . . . Children taught kindness to animals become not only more kind to animals, but to one another."

Angell's passion was inflamed in 1868, when he read a newspaper account of an endurance race in which two horses, each pulling two riders, were brutally galloped full speed for more than forty miles over rough terrain, with no rest or water. Both ultimately collapsed; in the guise of sport, the two horses were literally raced to death. Angell was so horrified by the cruelty that he wrote a blistering letter of protest to the *Boston Daily Advertiser*. The letter caught the attention of a Boston socialite and animal advocate named Emily Appleton, who had hopes of founding an SPCA in Massachusetts similar to one founded in New York by Henry Bergh. With Appleton's financing and Angell's legal expertise, the Massachusetts Society for the Prevention of Cruelty to Animals (MSPCA) was launched March 31, 1868, with Angell as the first president, a position he held until his death in 1909.

Laying the Groundwork

Within a few short months of the MSPCA's launch, Angell managed to raise $13,000 and add 1,600 new members to the organization. He drafted and achieved passage of Massachusetts' first general anticruelty act, and by 1871, similar anticruelty statutes had been enacted in states across the country. Animal protection societies sprang up in twenty-four American cities, and the movement was gaining political traction and increasing public support. Angell also connected with other humane activists in Europe.

From the beginning, Angell cleverly leveraged the cache of some of the organization's more high-profile enthusiasts, like John Quincy Adams II, Ralph Waldo Emerson, William G. Weld, and Henry Saltonstall. Among the first board members of the organization, they regularly gathered to devise ways of bringing visibility to the cause and paving the way for legislative reform. These powerful movers and shakers helped lay the groundwork for a revolution in how society views and treats animals.

At the core of Angell's vision was education, with a focus on teaching people of all ages and classes the principles of kindness, compassion, and respect for all life. He believed the future of the movement was in the nation's children. In 1881, he teamed up with Reverend Thomas Timmins to launch Bands of Mercy, a nationwide network of humane-education youth clubs in which school children pledged to be kind to all living creatures and protect them from abuse. Within two years, there were hundreds of Bands of Mercy across the country, with membership of close to 250,000 girls and boys. By the early twentieth century, there were reportedly more than 27,000 Bands of Mercy.

In 1886, the MSPCA opened its first official headquarters at 19 Milk Street in Boston. Three years later, Angell incorporated the American Humane Education Society (AHES), an organization working in partnership with the MSPCA that was designed "to carry unsectarian humane education gratuitously outside the State of Massachusetts, throughout the country and the continent, and by the employment of suitable agents to establish Bands of Mercy and Humane Societies wherever they are most needed."

In 1890, Angell published the first American edition of Anna Sewell's classic *Black Beauty*, and distributed two million free copies through the Bands of Mercy. Three years later, the AHES distributed the children's classic *Beautiful Joe*. Both books persuasively told stories from an animal's distinctive point of view. Angell himself, having given up the law to devote most of his energies to the cause so dear to his heart, continued his own

forms of persuasion. He lobbied tirelessly and passionately, often chastis-
ing in print public figures (including Theodore Roosevelt) whom he felt
were behaving inhumanely toward animals. Animal rights pioneer Henry
Bergh wrote to him: "I have seen you spoken of by the Press here, as 'an
Angell of mercy.' You are earning the title."

Toward the end of his life, Angell's health began to suffer dramatically,
yet he continued to work from home, overseeing administrative duties and
submitting editorials, dictating one to his secretary just hours before his
death. On March 16, 1909, he died peacefully at the age of eighty-five. By
the time of his death, Angell had sparked the establishment of more than
seventy thousand Bands of Mercy, and according to his *New York Times*
obituary, he was known domestically and abroad as "the friend of animals."

Thousands lined the streets for Angell's burial cortege from Boston to
Watertown's Mount Auburn Cemetery. The solemn, affecting procession
included thirty-eight workhorses with mourning rosettes on their halters,
led by the thirty-five-year-old award-winning workhorse Old Ned.

Three years later, the MSPCA erected the Angell Memorial Fountain
in honor of its founder. More than simply commemorative, the fountain
reflected Angell's lifelong ethos; forty-three years earlier, in 1869, Angell
had raised funds to build Boston's very first public drinking fountains,
including twenty for animals. Designed by Peabody and Sterns and located
in Boston's Post Office Square, this new memorial's tall flagstaff, which
included a gilded copper eagle on top, arose from a stone basin ringed by
lion-head spouts. Each spout of the 1912 Angell Memorial Fountain spewed
water into the stone basin for the city's thirsty, hard-working horses.

CHAPTER 2

The Vision of Dr. Francis H. Rowley

ONE HUNDRED YEARS AGO, the plight of homeless, abandoned, and abused animals was still a rather radical social cause. At the time, the commitment to the humane treatment of animals was primarily geared toward preventing mistreatment, especially to beasts of burden.

An even more innovative idea was the concept of conscientiously promoting animal health as a fundamental component of welfare. That philosophy is at the heart of the MSPCA–Angell. In 1915, the MSPCA opened Angell Memorial Animal Hospital, one of the first veterinary hospitals connected to a humane organization. Its torchbearer was the MSPCA's second president, Dr. Francis H. Rowley.

After George Angell's death in 1909, Dr. Francis H. Rowley (1854–1952) was chosen in 1910 to be the MSPCA's second president, a position he would fill for three and a half decades. In contrast to the fiery, impassioned Angell, with his long silver beard, Rowley was balding and short, with round gold-rimmed glasses and a kindly manner. The father of four, he was the very picture of paternal benevolence.

A gentleman and a scholar, Rowley was a Baptist minister who had served congregations in Pennsylvania and Illinois as well as several in Massachusetts, including the historic First Baptist Church of Boston (1890–1910). Long committed to a number of humanitarian efforts, and an ardent peace advocate, Rowley also served as the secretary and vice president of the American Humane Association and was a director of the Animal Rescue League. Through his many endeavors, he saw firsthand the special joy and comfort animals could bring to their owners, and he backed up his vision with a unique perspective.

While most veterinarians of the day primarily took care of horses, which were still valuable service animals integral to daily life, Rowley had the vision to foresee a need for a center that could treat companion animals. He felt such a center should also be dedicated to furthering the service and science of animal welfare. He explained, "The idea before us is to advance to the limit of our power the whole practice of veterinary medicine and surgery in New England; to set an ever-higher standard, and to assist all members of this important profession in establishing their work on the best possible level."

Shortly after taking over as the MSPCA's president, Rowley purchased the organization's first motorized ambulance to serve horses. (Horses still dominated city streets, including pulling non-motorized ambulances.) Rowley also began pushing for a first-class treatment destination for the ambulance to bring the ailing horses. Noting that a number of animal hospitals had already sprung up abroad as well as in New York City, Rowley pressed for the MSPCA to build its own veterinary hospital in Boston. He wrote, "This is the latest phase of humane work. It is one more step forward. Once it was just to protect the animal from its tormentors. Now, to care for him when sick or injured, if his value to his owner warrants it, is demanded by a deepening sense of what humanity and kindness mean."

So construction began on the $200,000 brick and limestone building at 180 Longwood Avenue that was to house the MSPCA's myriad activities as well as a world-class veterinary hospital—all under one roof. Located in the heart of Boston's medical district, Angell Memorial Animal Hospital opened to invited visitors with great fanfare on February 25, 1915. It was dedicated to George T. Angell, "Apostle of Humanity to Animals," and its mission was to provide the best medical care for animals and to advance the practice of veterinary medicine. The *Boston Post* proclaimed, "It is a rare distinction that Boston now has—the possession of the best and largest animal hospital in the world. It is a very appropriate distinction, also, for here has the sentiment of mercy for the creatures that cannot help themselves been effectively fostered for years."

Cat paying the bill

A horse is accompanied to Angell in an ambulance specially designed to carry large farm animals

CHAPTER 3

Growth of the MSPCA—
And a Trailblazing Hospital
Opens Its Doors

WITH WORLD WAR I raging overseas and the United States on the verge of declaring war on the German Empire, Rowley increased efforts to promote a peaceful, humanitarian position both in his politics and in his activism at home. In 1917, the MSPCA opened its first permanent animal shelter at Nevins Farm in Methuen, Massachusetts. With Rowley at the helm, the MSPCA's reach was felt internationally as well over the following decades.

In 1927, the American Fondouk was established in Fez, Morocco. The Fondouk is a full-service animal hospital that treats more than twenty-two thousand animals annually—all free of charge. The MSPCA has managed the Fondouk for more than eighty years. When American tourist Amy Bend Bishop visited Morocco in the late 1920s, she was horrified by the harsh reality of the conditions of animals, mostly working equines, in Fez. Mrs. Bishop urged Dr. Francis Rowley and Sydney Coleman, a prominent New York animal activist, to build a refuge for the animals of Morocco. Respectively, Dr. Rowley and Mr. Coleman served as the first and second presidents of the Fondouk, bringing aid to thousands of animals in Morocco. Years later, Sydney's grandson, Bob Coleman, would take the helm as Fondouk president. To this day, the MSPCA is deeply involved in the veterinary care of Moroccan working animals, sometimes sending veterinarians from Angell to consult and work with the Fondouk staff.

The MSPCA also supports animal welfare efforts in Turkey, through its Alice Manning Trust. This effort, which began in 1937, was a result of confidence in the medical excellence of the veterinarians at Angell.

In 1989, Angell's longtime Chief of Staff, Dr. Gus Thornton, stepped from that position into the presidency of the MSPCA, initiating fourteen years of visionary leadership. He maintained that the best outcome for animals would lie in changing the attitudes and behaviors of the public. Under Dr. Thornton, the MSPCA intensified its effort to deal with the increasingly complex needs of animals in a rapidly changing society, and also stepped in to help set up shelters and provide education programs internationally, providing veterinary care, medicine, and books. And in 1993, the MSPCA celebrated its 125th anniversary.

During these decades, Angell Memorial Animal Hospital was flourishing as well. In addition to fostering the development of new techniques and procedures for veterinary diagnostics and treatment, the hospital created landmark internship and residency programs, and the publication of groundbreaking medical texts and papers allowed Angell's innovators and visionaries to share their knowledge and skills with the world at large.

Angell Takes Flight: A Groundbreaking Hospital Is Opened

Angell's primary focus in 1915 was to tend to the workhorses still so vital to city life, pulling delivery wagons, carriages, and all kinds of service vehicles. The hospital not only had ambulances to bring ailing horses in, but special operating tables onto which a horse could be safely strapped, with dedicated recovery stalls for comfortable convalescence.

However, from the very beginning, the hospital also had a Small Pet Department that served the variety of animals that people kept for companionship and pleasure. In addition to surgical and dental/irrigation rooms, there were separate wards for cats and dogs. The *Greenfield Recorder* noted,

> Rooms that afford every protection to the convalescent creature speak for the advanced notion of the duty that men have come to own towards the dumb creatures. Most significant of all in this new establishment is the evidence it supplies of the changed thought of men as to animals. It is the one right and fitting monument to George T. Angell, who devoted his life and extraordinary talents to developing the humane thought.

At the end of the hospital's first week, Rowley wrote,

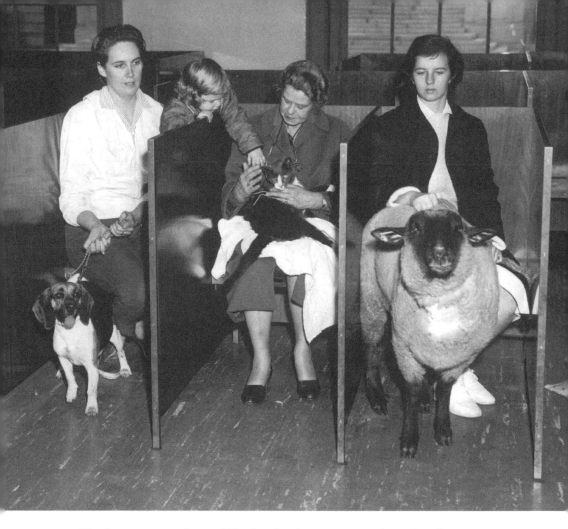

The diverse patients that could be found in the waiting room during Angell's early days

Today eighteen patients were brought to the Dispensary and eight small animals left for treatment; and ten operations performed. We have already eight horses in the Hospital. We hope to do a great deal of free work for those in straightened circumstances. The first week has seen a good proportion of all our cases attended to without charge. We are advertising the Free Dispensary as widely as possible, and it looks as if the hours devoted to this special service would soon be so crowded that they would have to be lengthened. The Small Pet Department starts on its career auspiciously with nearly thirty boarders. One of our most difficult problems is to attend to the many visitors who want to look through the building.

Over the first five weeks of operation, the hospital tended to 250 dogs, 124 cats, and 7 birds, in addition to 69 horses. The hospital administration reported, "We have had many very kind and wholly unsolicited letters from owners of animals which have been treated, expressing their great satisfaction with the treatment received and the skillful service of the veterinarians."

By the end of its first year, Angell had treated 4,382 animals. No one was turned away because of an inability to pay. By the next year, the annual count had more than doubled—to 10,813—and the hospital seemed destined to serve more and more animals each year. Rowley wrote,

> . . . the expediency of such an institution as an animals' hospital was denied by some when it was first proposed, but today it is well recognized that the practical illustration of the humane idea demands that a place be provided where animals may receive proper medical and surgical treatment. Like all new ideas, this one has its opponents—but its adherents are increasing every day.

After World War I, as the automobile became cheaper and more accessible, the sight of horses began dwindling on city streets. At Angell, this meant a gradual shift from equine medicine to an emphasis on treating small animals. For Angell's veterinarians, this changeover sparked new ways of thinking and breakthroughs in diagnostics, procedures, and treatments. Angell became one of the first clinical settings to institute a sterile environment for the surgery of small animals. With the MSPCA's support and state-of-the art equipment, the hospital developed a clinical diagnostic laboratory and a necropsy room. The incorporation of veterinary nurses and 24-7 care, unknown in other clinical settings, became regular features at the hospital.

During its first few decades, Angell was a beacon of progressive veterinary medicine, obtaining more and more sophisticated equipment and pioneering new approaches to animal care. Angell was the first American animal hospital to use fluoroscope and X-ray machines. Veterinarians at Angell continued to refine surgical and sterilization techniques, and

Two boys bring their puppy to the first Angell Memorial Animal Hospital at 180 Longwood Avenue

Post–World War I, smaller household pets such as dogs and cats became more common in the waiting area at Angell

developed the use of barbiturate intravenous anesthetics. In 1933, Angell surgeon Dr. Erwin F. Schroeder adapted a human technique for repairing broken bones to heal fractures in cats and dogs. The landmark Schroeder-Thomas Splint immobilized an injured animal's joint while the fractured leg bones healed, yet still allowed mobility, unlike the wooden splints that previously had been used. Early on, these special splints for small cats and dogs were made of coat hangers and steel brace wire from fences. Rods of aluminum alloy were used for larger dogs. Angell also documented a case of one frisky, two-month-old Guernsey calf who, after quenching her thirst, tried to hurdle her drinking trough—and missed. Brought into Angell, she was splinted and was back on her feet in good order.

In the late 1930s and '40s, chest surgery and cataract operations became commonplace at the hospital, and Angell's first clinical diagnostic laboratory was opened. In 1940, Angell launched the first veterinary intern training program, and in 1945, one of Angell's most influential veterinarians, Dr. Gerry Schnelle, authored the first English language textbook in veterinary radiology, *Radiology in Canine Practice* (The North American Veterinarian, 1945). Both landmark initiatives enabled a greater reach of the hospital's groundbreaking work.

In 1942, Angell established the first animal isolation ward to reduce the spread of infection among animals. Using cases from the isolation ward, Angell was later able to begin a program in distemper research. In 1945, Angell pioneered the concept of admitting patients, offering around-the-clock nursing care for animals who were too compromised to return home immediately after treatment. At the time, "nurses" referred to a variety of veterinary staff and attendants who mainly gave pills and shots, but given the need for more staff trained in a range of services for overnight care, Angell soon began an official nurses training program. Over the years, nurses have become a critical component of Angell's staff. Committed to the hospital's mission of compassionate care, they have become adept at a wide range of duties and skilled with a variety of sophisticated equipment.

Also in 1945, a highly regarded Angell surgeon named Dr. Rudolph Schneider performed a completely new operation that repaired a diaphragmatic hernia in a dog. He used a revolutionary technique that he developed incorporating, of all things, a bicycle pump. The procedure was filmed and shared with other veterinarians around the country. And in 1948, an adorable Dachshund named Bonnie became Angell's one-millionth patient.

Innovative Internship

One of Angell's most groundbreaking innovations of the era was the establishment of a veterinary intern training program. By bringing in young veterinarians from around the world to hone their skills under the guidance of Angell's expert staff, the hospital initiated a level of outreach and connection with the animal medical community that remains the gold standard even today. Interns as well as veterinary students (externs) and residents take advantage of Angell's large, extraordinarily diverse caseload to experience the breadth and depth of veterinary care.

In the 1940s, the MSPCA established the first veterinary internship program in the United States at Angell to help advance the practice of veterinary medicine. Residency and continuing education programs were added in subsequent years. Since the 1940s, Angell has taught more than 600 interns and 160 residents, who have carried best practices learned at Angell out into the larger world of veterinary medicine, practicing all over the United States and around the world. Some Angell graduates have extended their reach beyond veterinary medicine and into the world of animal welfare, often finding that the two spheres are inextricably interwoven. Angell now offers residencies in cardiology, avian and exotic medicine, emergency and critical care, internal medicine, and surgery.

The Intern Intensive

After four years of college, five years as director of the MSPCA Animal Care and Adoption Center in Boston, and another four years in veterinary school at Tufts, Dr. Meagan Rock could have gone right into private practice. But instead, she opted for what might be the most rigorous thirteen months of her life, as an Angell Animal Medical Center intern. "I really wanted to be in that learning environment, to get a year under my belt where I wouldn't be expected to have all the answers," Rock says, "where colleagues and technicians would know you're here to learn and grow and be pushed to be the best doctor you can be."

The internship gives young veterinary school graduates additional hands-on clinical experience under the guidance of experienced doctors. It is also the first step toward specialization, which requires three more learning years as a resident. At Angell, interns have a lot of primary case responsibility. "They're not glorified students," explains Dr. Megan Whelan, who was an Angell intern herself in 2003 and has been Angell's Director of Interns since 2008. "They are doctors, and they act like doctors, speaking with clients about things like overall health and financing. Most places don't do that, but we believe that's important, and most of our interns come here because of that."

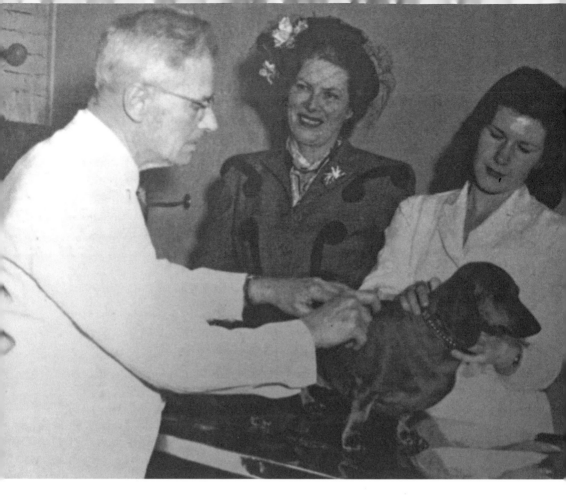

Dr. Erwin Schroeder, Nurse Dorothy Broderick, and owner Mrs. James Denning with Bonnie the Dachshund, Angell's one millionth patient

Interns generally work six days a week, twelve to sixteen hours a day, and their entire thirteen months is mapped out from day one. The program rotates each intern through a variety of shifts and services, including internal medicine, emergency/critical care, neurology, ophthalmology, cardiology, oncology, surgery, avian/exotic medicine, and radiology/ pathology. Then there's the prized "Brum-tern," a rotating position affording the opportunity to work one-on-one with one of Angell's most highly regarded veterinarians, Dr. Douglas Brum. "He's an exceptional doctor, and interns can learn how to handle large caseloads, manage long-term patients, communicate with clients, and be with a doctor seeing scheduled appointments," Whelan says.

A large part of the intern's job is emergency intake, which Rock says has an inherent unpredictability. "You could have a really easy day or a really bad one, and that unpredictability can be a challenge. But I can't think of a better place to learn in terms of the variety of the caseload. From day one you're constantly asked to make decisions for yourself and your patients. Even though you have a lot of help and support from an incredible staff of doctors and nurses, you realize very quickly it comes down to what you think is right. At first that's inspiring. It's exciting to finally be able to do something with all that knowledge you've acquired. But it's also terrifying. There's so much you don't know, and you have to respect the learning curve. Angell teaches what you know and what you don't know pretty quickly."

That rigor and pace can be daunting. "There's no real break," Rock explains. "You're constantly working and have to get very comfortable working at such a high level with the amount of work we do for each patient—the diagnostics, the workup, the paperwork. It requires a lot of mental and emotional energy, so there's sometimes very little left for yourself. I just went for a run for the first time in three months. You have to put a lot to the side, but you know it's only for a year."

And the skills Rock is acquiring translate beyond medicine. "Looking back from day one, I see myself now able to feel more confident—how I think about things, how I process information and work up problems is more efficient and fluid. I really appreciate how important it is to be open-minded and keep learning, to make sure I'm constantly striving to know what's the best practice. Angell is the kind of place that if you let the smallest ball drop, someone will notice, so you learn not to do that."

For Rock, an internship in Angell's prestigious, highly competitive program was the brass ring. Angell was the first veterinary hospital in the world to launch an intern program, starting in 1940. Initially, the program was relatively informal, with only one or two participants. But as it grew, serving more young doctors and offering a greater range of specialty medicine disciplines, it established the hospital as an international teaching facility.

Dr. Susan Cotter, acclaimed for her groundbreaking work in feline leukemia during her fifteen years at Angell, came to the hospital as an intern in 1966. Growing up in Illinois, she was only thirteen when she saw an

Meagan Rock,
former Angell Animal
Medical Center
intern

article about a special veterinary hospital in Boston and decided Angell was where she wanted to go. The only woman in a class of eight enthusiastic and idealistic interns, she recalls the tight camaraderie engendered by long hours and a supportive, accessible staff who gave interns room to grow. "We did a lot on our own and learned a lot by problem solving in the middle of the night."

Angell surgeon Dr. Mike Pavletic was in the last intern class in the hospital's Longwood location in 1975. "On any given night, an intern was the *only* doctor on duty to see clients through the night," he recalls. "That same intern also performed most of the emergency procedures and oversaw cases in the critical care unit. After finishing a procedure, you would run downstairs to see clients, sometimes several waiting to be seen in the early morning hours. The following morning, we then got up to work a regular shift seeing appointments while also caring for the patients we admitted that night. It was brutal at times, no sleep for forty hours. But those hardships built strong bonds between intern mates—like the bond between combat soldiers."

Dr. Douglas Brum, who went through the program in 1985, has written about how dramatically the program has changed over the years. He writes in an alumni newsletter,

> I remember going on morning rounds in that small crowded Intensive Care Unit (ICU), surrounded by cages and treatment tables with dozens of doctors, nurses, and students all jammed into a space not even a quarter of the size of the space we have now. In fact, the old ICU is where we currently perform endoscopy and recover some post-op animals. Everything happened at the same time, too; nurses doing treatments, triage, and emergencies. Boy, did we learn quickly.

Through exposure to many different doctors, he learned a variety of approaches for tackling medical issues:

> I remember Gus Thornton's large hands somehow being able to palpate the subtlest abnormalities on our patients. I remember Neil Harpster not making you feel stupid when he noticed the abscess on that cat's leg that you were working up for a fever of unknown origin. I remember Rhea Morgan's incredible efficiency. I remember Mike Bernstein, just solving my problems. Then there would be those interesting late nights listening to Keith Richter and Allen Sisson arguing. . . . They had a "unique" way of bantering with each other. Let's just say they both had very strong opinions!

Today's intern system is considerably more humane, and Angell's internship training program remains one of the most prestigious in the world, providing a rigorous clinical experience for sixteen doctors each year. "Things have changed a lot at Angell, but in many ways it remains the same," Brum believes. "The interns still work their tails off and learn a ton. They become part of Angell tradition, and they become a family. People help each other out."

In fact, one special aspect of Angell's program is mentoring that allows those interested in specialty education to be matched with a doctor who can offer individual guidance and advice, not just on clinical matters but on practical concerns such as job placement and paper writing. "Most private practices don't offer that," Whelan says. "We see a lot of doctors who've [gone elsewhere] and come back here. It's a very tight-knit group."

While hours for Angell interns are long and hard, often starting early and ending late, it's not all work, and Angell's large class affords a great deal of social connection and camaraderie. "The program is fun because there are a lot of traditions built in," says Whelan. "There's a Roast Night, when all the senior doctors roast the interns; there's a graduation party, a halfway party, a Super Bowl party, a picnic. It's a very hard year, so it's good to have things in the hospital to break up the year socially."

Dr. Katie Hogan, who graduated from the program in 2014 and is now a resident at the hospital, maintains that one of the most valuable characteristics that sets the Angell internship apart is the "unending support" interns receive, from people at the front desk and the client care coordinators to staff clinicians and residents. "Although we had been trained to have confidence and think independently, there was always someone willing to give us guidance when it was needed," she recalls.

Hogan also credits her fellow interns with helping her make it through the year. As she wrote in a recent volume of *Alumni News,*

> Sixteen of us, fresh out of veterinary school, all terrified and excited to finally be veterinarians. Not only have we established life-long friendships, we considered ourselves family since week one. We laughed (to the point of crying), we cried from exhaustion and seemingly impossible, frustrating days. More importantly, we learned from one another, supported one another. Ultimately, we were always there for one another. . . . They have become my best friends.

Three months from graduation, Meagan Rock thinks she will look back on her Angell internship as one of the best years of her life. "It's been an incredible, life-changing experience. I've learned a lot about myself and about medicine. It's grueling and exhausting, but a very rewarding year I will always cherish—aside from the few gray hairs!"

An Angell doctor examining a sailor's cat

CHAPTER 4

The Age of Specialization

AFTER THE END of World War II, with the country getting back on its feet, veterinarians at Angell began pioneering a range of specialties that allowed them to dig more deeply into some of the complexities of animal health. In addition, with all specialties housed under one roof, collaborative exchange and synergy greatly enriched the hospital's capabilities.

Several of Angell's top veterinarians became involved in establishing the specialty organizations (called *colleges* or *boards*) that certified practitioners. Dr. Peter Theran, who was an Angell veterinarian and administrator during his four decades at the hospital and was instrumental in the development of the American College of Veterinary Internal Medicine, explains, "The big three were Gerry Schnelle, who wrote the first book on canine radiology; Todd Munson, who broadly practiced internal medicine but also was interested in endocrinology, dermatology, and ophthalmology; and one of my mentors, Lawrence Blakely, who was a wonderful surgeon and teacher. These doctors were already specializing in areas of practice at a time when it wasn't common. They became very good at what they did even before specialties were developed or formalized." Blakely developed a technique of perineal hernia repair that is still considered the gold standard.

As veterinary specialties began to flourish, young animal doctors from around the world looked to Angell's pioneers for guidance, resulting in the development of the hospital's renowned residency program. Over the years, having talented young veterinarians spend three years developing their expertise in a given field has resulted in a rich cross-fertilization of ideas, knowledge, and techniques. As Chief of Staff Ann Marie Greenleaf can attest, "Residents bridge the gap of knowledge between the interns and the senior staff and represent another group of talented individuals whose

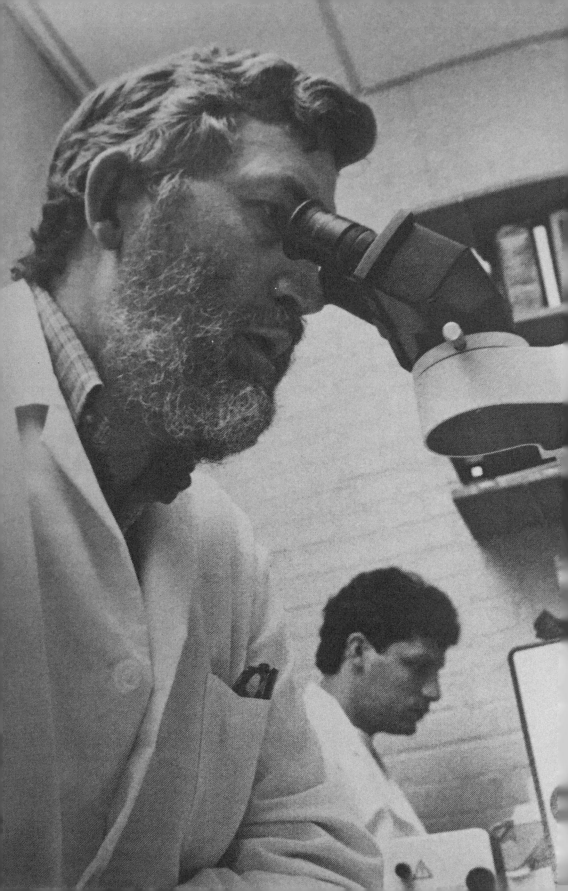

knowledge can be accessed by interns and support staff at all hours of the day and night. They challenge the senior staff to continue to grow and develop as they plumb the recent veterinary literature and ask questions that may not have answers yet. Questions without easy answers spark a quest to do research or develop a new technique or treatment to advance veterinary medicine."

Medical Detectives: Pathology

In the 1930s, Angell's first clinical diagnostic laboratory was opened, and within a few years, Angell became the first private hospital to create a dedicated pathology department in which tissue could be studied on the spot and necropsies could be performed to further the understanding of animal health issues. Mimicking the procedures of human pathology, the department was able to examine tissue microscopically and analyze blood, body fluids, and waste products, all in the service of investigating diseases and identifying organisms that could be hazardous to pets and pet owners. "It was major as far as the quality of the practice," former Angell veterinarian and administrator Dr. Peter Theran asserts.

From the beginning, questions and answers, causes and effects drove the medical detective work of Angell pathologists, who discovered a host of new diseases and shared their findings through scientific articles and professional education forums. The department also became committed to providing direct information and advice to veterinarians outside the practice, and over time, the work of Angell had an international reach. As early as 1976, Dr. James L. Carpenter, then the head of Angell's Department of Pathology, told *The Boston Globe*, "The results of autopsies at Angell are recorded and used worldwide. We have veterinarians from throughout this country and Canada, and as far away as Holland and England, visit our pathology department for consultation."

From his days as an intern in 1961, Dr. Peter Theran remembers the weekly clinical pathology conference, in which the clinical details of a case were presented and the veterinarians on hand would debate their theories of what might have led to a given medical issue. "Then pathology would

Dr. James L. Carpenter, former head of Angell's Department of Pathology present their answers. It was modeled after [a practice at] Massachusetts General Hospital, and it was a wonderful teaching experience."

A training program for pathologists was created at Angell in 1960 by Dr. T. C. Jones, and in 1970, the hospital started a residency program in pathology. Clinical research at Angell also has resulted in discoveries relating to human health, such as a form of muscular dystrophy in male cats similar to its counterpart in humans.

Today, Angell's pathology department is cutting edge as one of the only veterinary hospitals in the Northeast to offer in-house clinical and anatomic pathology services, providing veterinarians a quick assessment of biopsy specimens and lab tests, from blood and urine analysis to endocrine levels and parasite diagnostics. This rapid processing facilitates more efficient diagnosis and treatment. For critical-care patients, point-of-care testing "cage-side" allows for 24-7 test results and support for monitoring levels such as blood gas, electrolytes, and clinical chemistry. Angell clinical and anatomic pathologists also continue to be in demand as consultants, offering their expertise to outside practices around the country via detailed reports and case comments. During pathology rounds, select cases are reviewed for open discussion among pathologists, general practitioners, veterinary specialists, residents, interns, and veterinary technicians. And pathology supports the work of the MSPCA's law enforcement team by offering expert forensic medicine in cases under investigation. For Angell's medical detectives, the search for causes and cures is an ongoing mission.

Looking Inward: Radiology

In 1895, German physicist Wilhelm Conrad Röntgen accidentally discovered an electromagnetic wave that could penetrate varying kinds of matter to cast an image. A week after his discovery, he used his discovery to take an image of his wife's hand, which showed her bones as well as her wedding ring. He coined the term "X-radiation," with "X" referring to "unknown," and within a year, the practice of using X-rays for finding broken bones and other abnormalities had spread rapidly within the world of medicine. Within months, the fluoroscope was invented to provide a continuous beam of radiation that allowed for viewing an image in real time.

While it wasn't until around World War II that X-ray technology was routinely integrated into veterinary practice, doctors at Angell had the foresight to realize its potential for animal diagnosis and treatment even earlier. Dr. Larry Kleine, Angell's first Director of Radiology, recalls, "When I came to Angell in 1967, I went back through all the old images and the oldest I could find were from 1939." But they weren't done at Angell—the hospital had sent clients, probably sub rosa, to Brigham and Women's hospital, where sympathetic doctors or technicians had provided the service for someone's beloved pet. By 1950, X-rays had become an essential diagnostic tool for veterinarians.

One of veterinary radiology's most ardent and insightful champions was Angell's Dr. Gerry Schnelle, who made a huge impact on the organization during his impressive tenure as both a veterinarian and an administrator, including Chief of Staff (1950–1966). Colleague Dr. C. Lawrence Blakely remembers "Ask Schnelle" was a frequent refrain around the hospital during his tenure, reflecting the respect and confidence the veterinarian inspired. "Few of us left his office without receiving some helpful suggestion, if not a solution, to our problems," Blakely wrote "He was an outstanding diagnostician at a time when today's sophisticated laboratories were just a dream." Happiest in the clinic, Schnelle was a tireless worker with a legendary ability to calm even the unruliest animal with his quiet, gentle approach.

According to Kleine, Schnelle wrote more than one hundred scientific articles that were filled with "unique insights and perceptive judgments that were often far in advance of the remainder of the profession." Schnelle served on numerous editorial boards and authored the first English-language textbook in veterinary radiology. Kleine adds, "His was the original description of canine hip dysplasia (1935). And he was among the first to recognize both the hazards and potential usefulness of radiology as a diagnostic tool in small animal medicine."

Schnelle also was a renowned speaker not only to national and international veterinary groups, but also to organizations dedicated to human medicine, such as the American Roentgen Ray Society and the New England Roentgen Ray Society. He was a founder of the American College of Veterinary Radiology, and Angell—as well as the University of Pennsylvania School of Veterinary Medicine—named suites in his honor.

In 1967, Angell hired Kleine to develop the hospital's first dedicated Department of Radiology. At the time, radiology was relegated to one standard machine capable of routine work and static images, one technician, and a file room. Kleine was empowered to establish a state-of-the-art facility, which he says was as good as most human hospitals of the day. "Our caseload went way up because doctors realized they had a way to take a better look at a situation and figure out the best possibilities for diagnosis, treatment, and follow-up, to make sure things were healing properly," Kleine says. "And as a referral center, we saw a lot of unusual cases."

When the hospital moved to Jamaica Plain in 1976, the new facility afforded a huge increase in working space. As more technologically sophisticated equipment gradually became more available, the department added digital imaging and MRI and CT machines and incorporated ultrasound and radio isotopes, changing its name to Diagnostic Imaging. Over the years, the department's facility to let doctors see underneath the skin has enabled remarkable achievements in diagnosis and treatment. It's also revealed a few surprises.

Unidentified Foreign Objects

One Angell veterinarian knew that a dog had choked down something he shouldn't have. The doctor needed to know exactly what the object was in order to decide whether it would pass naturally, could be grabbed by an endoscope, or would have to be surgically removed. Oh so carefully he threaded the endoscope down the anesthetized dog's throat, the lighted camera showing healthy pink tissue as it moved down the esophagus. Then, as the scope passed into the dog's stomach, he saw it—the bright smiling face of Elmo staring back at him. The dog had swallowed a toy statue of one of *Sesame Street*'s most famous denizens.

Any vet, and most pet owners, will tell you that animals can be very indiscriminate eaters, especially dogs. Angell clinicians have seen more than their fair share of quickly hoovered non-food objects, from string, which sounds harmless but can actually pose a big threat of cutting into the intestinal tract, to needles, knives, and teriyaki sticks. "Those can be

A pet goose gets ready for an X-ray

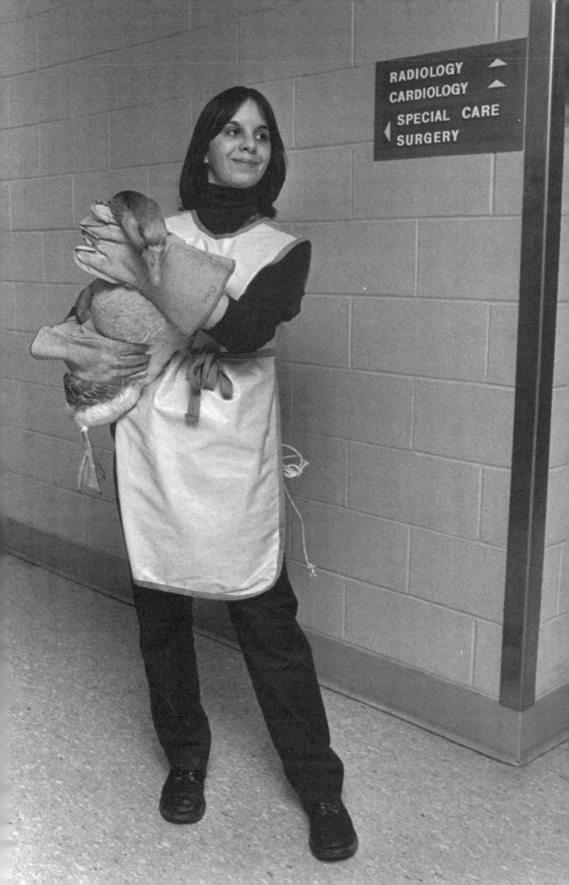

RADIOLOGY
CARDIOLOGY
SPECIAL CARE
SURGERY

particularly nasty," says Angell surgeon Mike Pavletic. "I have taken them out of the chest and abdomen as they migrate."

Pavletic cites a litany of other odd items Angell doctors have removed, including underpants, stones, peach pits, corn cobs, pacifiers, a perfume bottle, and Gorilla Glue. "It's interesting material when swallowed," he says. "It expands into a Styrofoam-like cast of the internal stomach."

The list goes on. And there's a story from decades ago, when long-time Angell surgeon and Chief of Staff Paul Gambardella operated on a baby harbor seal from the New England Aquarium. The creature had stopped eating, and when Gambardella opened him up, he saw why. Apparently aquarium visitors were in the habit of tossing coins into the seal pool for good luck, and the seal, perhaps thinking they were treats, quickly scarfed them down—nearly three hundred in all!

Hope for the Critically Ill

Even as veterinarians began focusing on a range of specialties, Angell's doctors remained flexible. Not only were they committed to a sound knowledge of general internal medicine for animals, but they were also comfortable with a wide range of procedures, techniques, and treatments. And as veterinary medicine became more and more sophisticated, animals once thought of as beyond hope were given greater chances of survival. With its ability to provide 24-7 care and monitoring of critically ill animals, Angell was one of the pioneers in the field of veterinary intensive care.

In 1959, Dr. Robert Cotton created a dedicated space in one of Angell's small wards for critical care. "It was a big deal at the time," recalls Dr. Peter Theran, who was an Angell internist for more than forty years as well as an administrator.

In the 1970s, Angell opened the first functional unit dedicated to intensive care, which allowed doctors to perform procedures and tests, then adjust treatments and monitor reactions on the spot. Under Cotton's direction, the unit had one nurse, seven cages, one exam table, and a large semi-portable ECG machine fondly referred to as "Big Bertha."

"His introduction of the use of intravenous catheters for fluid therapy

A dog receiving emergency care in Angell's Critical Care Unit

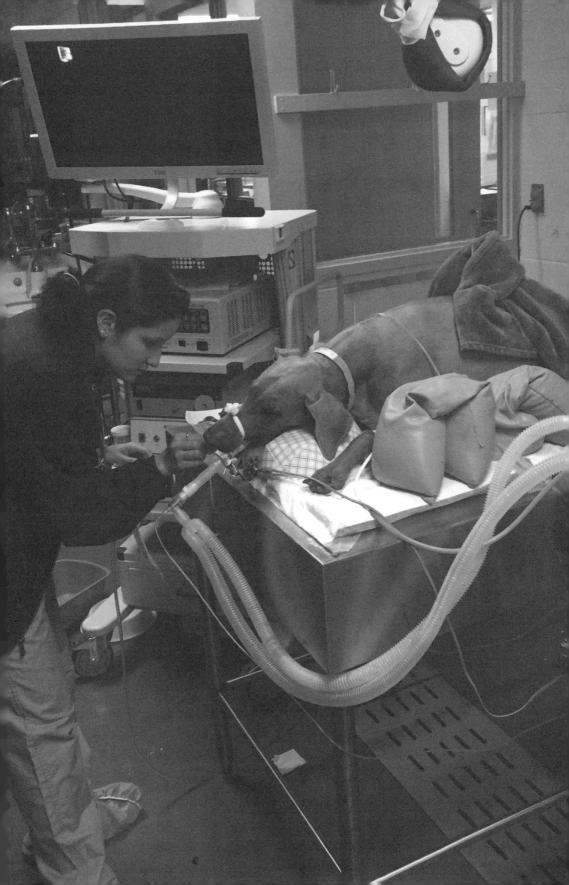

and measurements of central venous pressure helped many animals survive," explained Dr. Alicia M. Faggella, the Director of Intensive Care at Angell during the late 1980s and '90s. "Through Dr. Cotton's efforts, vital information on diseases was presented to the veterinary community."

When AMAH moved into its new building in 1976, the ICU was expanded to thirty-one cages, but the demand for accommodations for the seriously injured continued to grow. In 1986, Angell officially opened the Josephine M. Lilly Intensive Care Unit, which became the largest in the country for diagnosing, monitoring, and treating critically ill animals. In the next few years, the unit also became one of the most sophisticated in the United States, investing in top-of-the-line equipment to monitor patients' heart rates and rhythms without wires or clips and to record blood pressure noninvasively. Volumetric infusion pumps afforded precise control of intravenous fluid administrations. Temperature- and humidity-controlled oxygen enclosures provided an oxygen-rich environment for patients suffering from severe heart or respiratory diseases as well as trauma and shock. A portable cardiac defibrillator made it faster and easier to resuscitate an animal during arrest and to provide external pacing if a heart was beating too slowly.

Intravenous fluid therapy, which was a new technique when Angell's ICU first began, soon became the backbone of critical care treatment, with animals sometimes connected to several different IV lines at one time to provide vital blood products and maintenance fluids. In 1987, Angell integrated a nutritional management system call TPN (total parenteral nutrition) into critical care practice. Common in human medicine but rare in veterinary care at the time, the system involved intensive monitoring and very precise calculations to determine individual nutritional, fluid, and electrolyte needs. Formulations were often changed on a daily basis to adjust to a patient's fluctuating metabolic status. Other nutritional support systems were incorporated as well as tube feeding for patients unable to eat on their own, capitalizing on the vital role nutrition plays in healing and recovery.

Angell was also on the forefront of using blood products for ailing animals. During the ICU's early years, blood was rarely available for animals. But as intensive care medicine became more sophisticated, the use of blood products often became an essential part of treatment. Instead of routinely using whole blood, however, Angell used a more advanced process known as blood-component therapy, which allowed animals to receive either whole blood or only the specific blood component needed—packed red blood cells, plasma, or platelet-rich plasma.

Though the process was able to conserve blood, blood continues to be a precious commodity for sick animals. In April 1989, the MSPCA held the first-ever public blood drive for dogs and cats, which drew the participation of thirty-one pets. Now there are blood drives and blood banks for animals around the country.

As the hospital moved into the new millennium, the first brand-new mechanical ventilator was purchased, and the first class of Emergency and Critical Care residents began their three-year program. In 2001, Angell rebranded its ICU as the Critical Care Unit (CCU) to avoid confusion with the neighboring Intermediate Care Ward (ICW), which was designed for animals needing less aggressive care and monitoring. The acquisition of a portable ultrasound unit in 2007 made it possible for emergency staff to administer abdominal and thoracic ultrasounds for emergency and critical patients, further enabling quick diagnosis and treatment in life-threatening situations.

Today, Angell's Emergency and Critical Care service is the 24-7 pulse of the hospital, and the CCU is equipped with a full range of devices to monitor heart function, blood pressure, blood gas, and oxygen. Advanced techniques such as blood component therapy and peritoneal dialysis can come into play when needed, and Angell gets frequent referrals from practices with limited services.

"We do a good job of offering most of the ER services of a human hospital," says Emergency and Critical Care Director Kiko Bracker. "Angell is hugely emergency driven. We're sort of at the hub of the hospital, and because we have such a busy caseload, we're the engine for the other services. We get the sense of who needs to go to which specialty, to get the right patient to the right doctors."

At any hour of the day, 365 days a year, veterinarians from all around New England can send pets suffering from life-threatening trauma and disease to Angell for expert care, just as a neighborhood family can walk into the emergency clinic with an ailing cat in their arms and expect triage and treatment, compassion, and hope.

Critical Care Diary: Dr. Megan Whelan, Emergency and Critical Care Director and Service Director for Oncology and Avian and Exotic Medicine

3:30 A.M. I am awoken by my young son, Bryson. As he eats his breakfast, I check my e-mails, which include my nightly update from one of our residents regarding the status of the inpatients in the critical care unit. The subject line reads "crazy busy night." I see there are a number of sick patients admitted that will need attention when I arrive. I check to see how my own patients did overnight. I shower, leave the house with wet hair, which will dry only partially in the car.

6:30 A.M. I arrive at AAMC, boot up my computer, and look at my master list of things to do today. I put on my fanny pack, which holds my beeper, swipe card, hemostats, and some change for a drink later. I put a clean lab coat over my pale-blue scrubs, place my stethoscope around my neck, and I am ready to go upstairs to the unit. It is Friday, which means no scheduled meetings. It's nice to occasionally have a day without multiple meetings, which range from oncology to avian exotics to various committees. I walk around the unit and observe the patients in their cages to get a visual and familiarize myself with new arrivals. I sit down at the back table and begin to SOAP my own patients. (SOAP is an acronym that stands for "Subjective, Objective, Assessment, Plan," which standardizes a way a physical exam is performed and recorded.)

8 A.M. I am supposed to be at the Friday morning lecture on canine distemper, but the emergency list has exploded. A cat is triaged back to the unit with labored breathing due to abdominal distention. He is placed in oxygen as I set up to address the effusion in his abdomen. As I am draining the fluid, a large St. Bernard is triaged back. I do a quick physical and only find tachycardia. I scan his medical record quickly to see the most likely cause of his elevated heart rate. He has a history of megaesophagus—the muscles of his esophagus are not working properly—so he needs fluid resuscitation and chest radiographs to see if he has aspiration pneumonia. While I am working with him, a vomiting cat is placed in front of me. He is not moving, and with a quick abdominal palpation I deduce a urinary obstruction of the bladder. I write the stabilization orders and then put in the St. Bernard's radiograph request. One of the nurses alerts me that one

Dr. Megan Whelan,
Emergency and Critical
Care Director

of my own patients is now breathing with difficulty. He needs chest radiographs immediately. His radiographs are normal, but his skin is very red. I give him steroids for a presumptive severe allergic reaction. He is markedly improved within an hour. I have scheduled endoscopy and esophagotomy tube placement for a sixteen-year-old cat, but I want to aspirate his liver and spleen first.

8:45 A.M. I check my computer, which is always open. I receive about one hundred e-mails a day, ranging from quick fixes to major issues.

8:55 A.M. I walk into room 11 across from the CCU. It is the catch-all place to do things—eat, chat, monitor the "list," ask/offer an opinion.

9:00 A.M. Everyone is out of lecture, and we begin cage-side rounds on those cases that were seen on overnights. When those cases are squared away, I sit back in room 11 to type some discharges. An intern pops his head in and asks if I can review a case with him, and I make some recommendations. I walk down the hall and run into the managing technician supervisor, who tells me that today we are going to offer the oncology positions to two individuals whom we already conferenced on. I answer, "Great. This will definitely help this service."

10:30 A.M. An intern sits down next to me and begins talking about difficulties at home. I listen.

11:15 A.M. I go back to working on a feline patient that hasn't been eating for a week. On abdominal ultrasound the spleen looked abnormal; the aspirates showed a tumorous condition. The owner, an elderly gentleman, asked me yesterday to "fix" his cat. He had him for sixteen years and is "his only friend." Now I sit in the bereavement room with him. He does not want his cat to suffer, and he knows the diagnosis means poor quality of life. He makes the hard decision to euthanize. I stay with him through the process, making sure he is supported during this difficult time. I make him a clay paw print of his beloved friend to take home.

Barely even processing the prior ten minutes, I have to focus on my other inpatient, a small teacup Yorkie that only weighs two pounds and was diagnosed with hypoglycemia after vomiting at home. The owner only has enough money for one test, so I choose the one that I think will most likely yield the answer and am happy to get the result. She has giardia— a parasitic intenstinal infection—which is easy and inexpensive to treat. I make a mental note to tell the owner that this disease can be transmitted to humans and she needs to be sure her young children are washing their hands.

1:00 P.M. I look at my long list of outstanding things to do: write a lecture on canine heatstroke, read and correct a resident paper on escalator injuries, look over the alumni newsletter . . . The list keeps going, so I stop scanning. I consider running down the street to Whole Foods to sample something off the hot bar, and perhaps pick up a gallon of milk for my son, but the emergency list is picking up. As I savor my lunch, an intern asks me to feel the legs of a pet to confirm joint effusion.

1:30 P.M. On the way to the CCU, I see a container of what looks like paint on the table. I ask, "What is this?" My colleague says that is actually the urine from a Labrador in run #34. Interesting. The abdominal ultrasound will give the answer, I think.

4:30 P.M. I round out with the resident, reviewing the cases in the unit.

5:00 P.M. Time to go home. As I look at my checklist, which confirms I have spoken with all my owners, my patients are all tucked in, all their treatments are updated, and I have plans for them the following day, I venture downstairs. On my way out, I stop by my mailbox. There are two pieces of mail, including one from a student looking to do an externship that I need to sign off on. The other is a small envelope—a thank-you note from Tippy and her owner for taking good care of her. She is a sixteen-year-old Cairn that I treated last week for being unable to walk and being febrile. What a nice way to end the day.

7:30 P.M. Once Bryson is asleep, I give a final review of work e-mails and respond to anything urgent. I eat dinner with my husband and mother-in-law, and I consider working out or talking on the phone. But I know either will cut into time that could be used for sleeping. Wondering whether or not another snowstorm will appear overnight and force me to shovel in the early morning, I choose sleep.

Growth Spurt

By the 1960s, Angell's practice had grown enormously, both in sophistication and in the sheer volume of cases walking through the door. And for a while, some were arriving by shuttle as well. The MSPCA maintained an outpatient facility on Northampton Street in Roxbury, overseen by Dr. Rudy Schneider, and it provided a shuttle service for clients who didn't have transportation to get to the big hospital. "The dog or cat was placed in a carrier and escorted by a porter on the public trolley from the clinic to AMAH, where spaying or neutering was performed," remembers Dr. Larry Kleine, former Director of Radiology at Angell. "After an appropriate recovery, a porter returned the pet to the Northampton clinic, where the client could pick up their pet."

Angell's size also translated to a remarkable variety of cases, as more and more veterinarians began to refer clients to the hospital for specialized diagnosis and treatment. As former Angell veterinarian and administrator Dr. Peter Theran recalls, "While a veterinary school might see unusual cases like Cushing's disease two or three times a year, we would see thirty-five to forty cases, so clinicians at Angell had an experience in unusual diseases that was unmatched, and they became valuable contributors to the development of veterinary medicine at the time."

Angell's packed waiting room

New procedures for animals were developed and refined, such as total canine hip replacement and one of the first "doggie pacemakers." The use of nuclear medicine was integrated into Angell's arsenal of care, and the hospital began a residency program that further cross-fertilized the field of veterinary care. In 1969, renowned AMAH doctor Margaret L. Petrak published the first comprehensive book on bird care and disease, a book that was groundbreaking at the time and became the go-to avian manual for veterinary students and doctors. (The next avian medicine book wasn't published until 1986.)

As veterinary medicine began incorporating more and more technologically advanced equipment and highly trained employees, services at Angell became more expensive. "We could [no longer] afford to give away free services for people who couldn't afford it," recalls Theran. He remembers one staff meeting in the late '60s in which they discussed a variety of new initiatives that were expensive, but Dr. Gerry Schnelle, Chief of Staff at the time, expressed concern that the deficit was growing.

"We grappled with that for the next several decades," Theran says.

In the meantime, the hospital was in such demand that the waiting room was often completely packed, and lines of pets and their owners sometimes stretched out into the street. Theran recalls, "Angell saw pet owners from every walk of life, from affluent Beacon Hill to low income and everything in between. The people themselves were very interesting to interact with, and we were surrounded by specialists in every field. If I had a complicated neurology issue, I could get someone right down the hall, and that was a big deal. We taught residents and interns, and they taught us, bringing the latest news from the best veterinary schools. That comingling made it a wonderful environment."

"We did a lot of good work there," Kleine says, "but the place was kind of a high-crime zone and overnights were a nightmare." In addition, parking throughout the medical district was becoming nearly impossible, and the building itself, with its creaky elevator, was becoming more and more dilapidated and impractical. By the 1970s, a change was clearly in order.

PART TWO

A NEW BEGINNING, 1976–2000

THE AUGUST BRICK BUILDING in Boston's Jamaica Plain neighborhood that now houses the MSPCA–Angell has a long and storied history. At the turn of the nineteenth century, a building on what is now the parking lot of the facility at 350 South Huntington Avenue housed the kindergarten of the Perkins Institution and School for the Blind, the country's first such dedicated school. (The organization's groundbreaking work was put on the map when alumna Anne Sullivan was sent to instruct a young deaf and blind girl from Alabama, Helen Keller, whose accomplishments transformed how we think of people with disabilities.)

When Perkins moved to Watertown in 1912, the property was purchased by the House of the Angel Guardian orphanage and school, one of the city's major charitable institutions at the time. In the 1930s, the Cardinal O'Connell Seminary took over the property. On one side was a convent building, which, for some years, would house offices of the American Humane Education Society and the World Society for the Protection of Animals (now called World Animal Protection).

The Angell building at 350 South Huntington Avenue, Jamaica Plain, MA, circa 1976

CHAPTER 5

A Seminary Transformed

WHEN THE MSPCA and Angell moved into the building in 1976, many vestiges of seminary life were still evident, including dorm rooms and kitchens. There is also a luminous stained glass window of Francis of Assisi, adoring animals at his feet, that presides beneficently over Angell as the centerpiece of the hospital's research library. Originally part of the old building, the window was restored through donor contributions and set in its current wooden framework.

From the outside, the imposing structure looked a bit like a fortress in 1976, surrounded by a tall brick wall. Inside, however, the new facility soon became a mecca for pets in need from all around the city and beyond, and the increased space allowed the MSPCA room to further develop and expand the hospital as well as its humane services all under one roof.

Dr. Peter Theran, who came to Angell in 1961 as an intern and retired there in 2003, remembers being the last living soul in the old hospital on Longwood. "When we moved, we couldn't just close the old practice, so we kept functioning at Longwood," he says. "While everyone moved everything out, I was there with a cart of pharmaceuticals holding down the practice for that last twelve hours, till an ambulance came and took me and the cart to South Huntington."

It wasn't an inexpensive move—the building cost the MSPCA roughly $7 million. However, it resulted in the most extensive service center ever created by a humane society. Angell spokeswoman Mimi Steadman told *The Boston Globe* at the time, "To our knowledge, Angell Memorial is now the largest and best equipped animal hospital in the world, solely set up to service clients [owners] and patients [animals]."

In addition to the cost of the new facility, expenses were increasing as a whole in the field of veterinary medicine. Rapidly evolving technological advancements resulted in more sophisticated machines and devices. This necessitated more intensive training for staff and continued to increase the costs of pet diagnosis and treatment, further stressing the MSPCA's endowment and budget.

However, for the hospital and its staff, this move to a more expansive, accessible site was like a new beginning. Angell's Director of Radiology at the time, Dr. Lawrence "Larry" Kleine, recalls, "The new location gave us a huge increase in working space and parking, which allowed a major expansion of our services. Our caseload in radiology increased at approximately 20 percent each year thereafter."

Theran remembers, "The new place was large, sophisticated; it was organized better. The surgery, recovery, and CCU were all in one place; the pharmacy was in a good place. We had a chance to design it the way it should have been designed for that period."

In the ensuing decades, Angell continued to break new ground. From 1981 through 1985, Angell served as the small animal teaching hospital for Tufts University School of Veterinary Medicine while the school developed its own hospital. In 1983, Angell performed its first total hip replacement on a dog suffering from debilitating arthritis. In 1988, the hospital began incorporating nuclear medicine as a way to improve diagnostic and therapeutic treatment. The following year, twenty-six dogs and five cats participated in the first public blood drive ever held for pets, starting a trend that continues to this day at animal hospitals and humane centers around the country. Angell has also partnered with Massachusetts General Hospital for a "Human and Hound Blood Drive," encouraging donations of much-needed blood for both species.

In the 1990s, more specialty services were incorporated, including Avian and Exotics Medicine and Angell's Cancer Care Center, featuring onsite radiation therapy. In 1998, Angell opened a department of dentistry, and veterinarians at the hospital performed a successful feline kidney transplant.

Guiding the hospital into this fertile new era was one of the most revered veterinarians and administrators in Angell history, Dr. Gus Thornton.

Dr. Gus Thornton

A big bear of a man with a mild-mannered demeanor and a quiet sense of humor, Dr. Gus Thornton was one of the most influential leaders in the history of both Angell Animal Medical Center and the MSPCA. He started his forty-six-year career at Angell as a veterinary intern in 1957, and within a decade was promoted to the hospital's Chief of Staff, an office he held from 1966 to 1989. When he left that position, it was to become President of the MSPCA, guiding the organization into the new millennium before retiring at the end of 2002.

"Gus was a great veterinarian and humanitarian, a true leader in both fields, nationally and internationally," said current MSPCA–Angell President Carter Luke shortly after Thornton's death in 2010. "But I think his friends and colleagues remember him most for his heart. Gus cared so very deeply about animals and people. He was a kind and generous person, and he spent his life helping others."

A native of Oklahoma, Thornton was drawn to Angell by its renowned internship program, and he stayed on to practice internal medicine, becoming one of the founders of the American College of Veterinary Internal Medicine. Highly respected as a veterinarian, he became especially effective as Angell's Chief of Staff. Dr. Peter Theran, Thornton's best friend at the hospital for roughly four decades, recalls, "He was a quiet, unassuming man who had the contradiction of holding his personal feelings quite 'close to the vest,' but, at the same time, would become teary eyed at just about every intern graduation. As the Chief of Staff, he would be the emcee for the ceremony and would always give me a copy of his talk, and I'd have to sit in the front row so if he got teary and couldn't continue, I would come up and finish. He would get all emotional, and I think that's what endeared him to so many people. He had great affection for the organization and the people."

Thornton's benevolent leadership style was tempered by a determination to be just and fair. "He was a very modest man and tried to be inclusive of people's thoughts and opinions when making decisions," Theran said. "For many years, a sign with the old Harry Truman quote hung in his office—'There's no limit to what can be accomplished when it doesn't matter who gets the credit.' And he really believed that. That was how he approached his various leadership roles."

Under Thornton's direction, Angell instituted an internationally respected residency program and quadrupled its veterinary staff, who not only worked in the main hospital but also took their care giving to shelters and spay/neuter clinics. They also published more than four hundred scientific papers to share their expertise with other veterinarians. Angell built one of the nation's first veterinary Intensive Care Units and was a pioneer in veterinary nuclear medicine.

Another of Thornton's legacies was to ensure the humane treatment of animals used for research and testing, which had a complex and multifaceted history at facilities around the world. When the Animal Welfare Act of 1966 established regulations for the treatment of animals in research, in exhibition, in transport, and by dealers, every institution that used animals in research had to have a veterinarian overseeing their health and well-being. "Boston had many such institutions, and Angell had a lot of veterinarians," recalls Theran, who served as director of the Laboratory Animal Science Center at Boston University School of Medicine while also Angell's Assistant Chief of Staff. "Dr. Thornton felt that his veterinarians, on their own time, could serve in the role of the overseeing veterinarian at city research institutions, and, by doing so, could bring their humane background to the laboratory."

Thornton later created a new role for Theran, representing the MSPCA as head of the Center for Laboratory Animal Welfare (CLAW). In that position, Theran served as the animal welfare member on committees in the National Institutes of Health, the National Academy of Sciences, and on the boards of organizations such as Chimp Haven.

Thornton oversaw the hospital's move from its original building in the Longwood medical area into its larger, more sophisticated facility on South Huntington Avenue in 1976. While the move brought the MSPCA and Angell together in closer physical proximity, it also strained finances, and the hospital and the humane services sides of the organization didn't always agree on the same priorities. Dr. Larry Kleine believes, "People at Angell loved the place and each other, and they loved their work, but they sometimes felt like they didn't get enough support from the MSPCA. Salaries

Dr. Gus Thornton, former Angell Chief of Staff, 1966–1989, and former MSPCA President, 1990–2002

were low, people were under continuous pressure to produce more, and most were already working more than twelve hours a day. Gus was in the middle of that. He served at the pleasure of the MSPCA, but he had to keep his staff happy. It was a really tough job, but Gus bridged that gap. He had so much integrity. Nobody could have kept that place together but him. He was a rock in a maelstrom and the most wonderful guy. I never respected any veterinarian and administrator more. There was nobody like him."

After twenty-three years as Chief of Staff, Thornton was persuaded to take on the role of the presidency of MSPCA, a position in which he was further able to bring the two sides of the organization together, transforming it into what Theran calls a "benevolent society with good benefits that took care of its employees. The pace of practicing was pretty fast, especially if you were on overnight by yourself, but it's what you did, and it was intense but satisfying. And as far as people to work for, Gus was the best."

Thornton was the first veterinarian ever to head the MSPCA, and the hospital's staff, respecting his commitment and insight, began to buy into the organization's humane causes, such as spay/neuter campaigns and stronger pet shop regulations. During his tenure, Thornton championed legislation against trapping and animal abuse. The MSPCA established programs such as Living With Wildlife, a free spay/neuter clinic for low-income families, the Animal Disaster Relief Fund, the Center for Animal Laboratory Welfare, and Phinney's Friends, which helped people with HIV/AIDS take care of their pets. The MSPCA built new state-of-the-art adoption and veterinary facilities in Brockton, Martha's Vineyard, Nantucket, and Springfield.

The MSPCA extended its range internationally as well, working closely with the World Society for the Protection of Animals (WSPA), for which Thornton served as President for two years. He travelled around the globe, visiting not only countries where WSPA was working, but also the American Fondouk in Morocco and animal welfare effort in Turkey. The MSPCA provided supplies and funding to build sanctuaries for rescued dancing bears in Pakistan, Turkey, and India, and it helped protect Siberian tigers by equipping anti-poaching patrols. The organization delivered orthopedic surgical equipment to a wildlife rehabilitation center in Colombia and helped rescue wild and domestic animals caught in natural disasters and war zones.

Current MSPCA–Angell President Carter Luke believes Thornton's impact continues to be felt throughout the organization. "The MSPCA and Angell will always have his heart and soul firmly embedded in our walls and in our hearts. The world is a better, kinder, more humane place because of our dear friend."

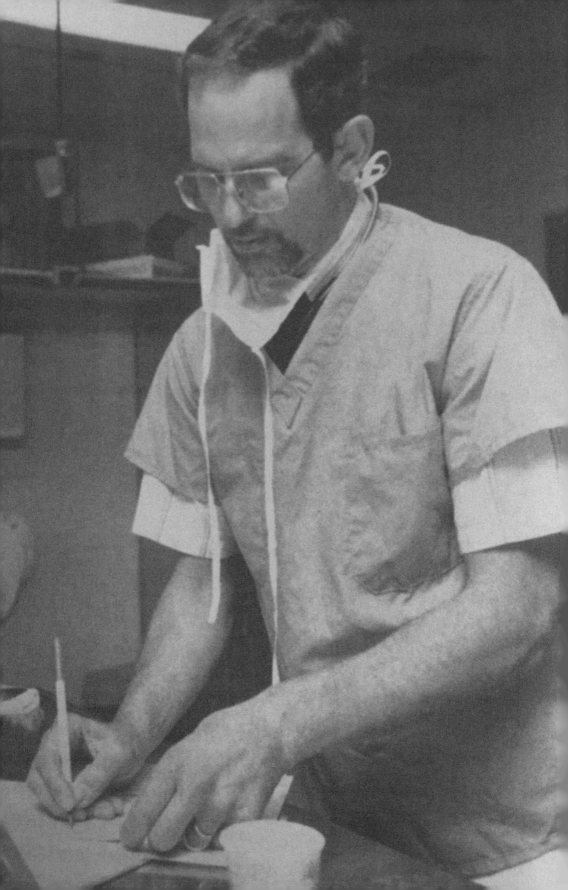

CHAPTER 6

Breaking New Ground

THE MSPCA–ANGELL'S new facility provided many of its burgeoning specialties with dedicated spaces with room to grow. At the time, the hospital's neurology department was the only one of its kind in New England, using spinal taps, biopsies, and X-rays as well as readings from electroencephalographs and electromyographs to diagnose abnormalities of the nervous system, many of which could then be controlled with medication. Avian and Exotic Medicine was established to cater not just to furry creatures, but also to those with feathers and scales. The hospital became a forerunner in the veterinary field with the establishment of a full-time Dentistry service, and the Oncology service opened its landmark Cancer Care Center. And two extraordinary women—Dr. Jean Holzworth and Dr. Susan Cotter—broke new ground in the study and treatment of feline diseases, including leukemia, hyperthyroidism, and infectious peritonitis.

It was during this time that the practice of cardiology at Angell really began to flourish as well. Shortly after moving into the new building, Angell was among the first veterinary hospitals in the world to implant a pacemaker into a dog to treat abnormal heart rhythms. It not only marked just how far veterinary science had progressed, it also reflected the remarkable transformation of Angell's cardiology department, which had, by all accounts, a rather modest start.

Matters of the Heart: Cardiology

"Humble beginnings is not an understatement," explains Dr. Neil Harpster, Director of Cardiology from the 1970s until 2005. "In the early days of

Dr. Neil Harpster, former Director of Cardiology

AMAH, the basic equipment for evaluating animals was a stethoscope, chest radiographs, and a Sanborn electrocardiograph machine. The staff of the section consisted of one person—a junior staff member."

And in fact, the department stayed a one-man show until the late 1960s, when a part-time cardiology consultant and a secretary/technician were added to the staff.

But in the mid-'70s, Harpster himself elevated Angell's cardio profile considerably. Assisted by Boston-based pacemaker specialist Dr. Paul Axelrod, he implanted a human pacemaker into a perky little dog named Muffin, pioneering a trans-venous procedure through the jugular rather than open chest surgery. At the time, Angell was one of only a handful of hospitals offering animals these electronic devices, which regulate the heartbeat to allow normal activity. Without pacemakers, animals with heart block were destined for lives of constant medication and severely restricted activity—or euthanasia. But in the decades since, veterinary cardiologists have used pacemakers to improve the lives not just of dogs, but also cats, horses, and even ferrets.

Angell cardiologist Dr. Rebecca Malakoff maintains, "Many people don't know that the very devices that have bolstered the health of humans with abnormal heart rhythms have actually been in use by the veterinary community for more than half a century. The pacemaker is just one of the many innovations modeled for human health care that the veterinary world has adapted to meet the ongoing care needs of pets."

Pacemaker implantations are only one facet of Angell's extensive cardiology practice today. The department deals with the diagnosis, treatment, and monitoring of a full spectrum of veterinary cardiac issues, from catheterizations and echocardiography to open-heart surgery. In fact, according to Angell's Director of Medical Services, cardiologist Dr. Nancy Laste, veterinary cardiology is very similar to human cardiology with two notable exceptions: Animals don't tend to get coronary artery disease, which is the leading cause of human death in the United States; and third-party payment (insurance) is relatively rare. "Our challenges lie in trying to be good at lots of different things that would be specialization roles in the

Dr. Rebecca Malakoff, veterinary cardiologist

human medical world, and to provide the interventions that are needed while remaining at least quasi affordable," she says.

That attitude is reflected throughout the hospital. Doctors act zealously to pinpoint the cause of an animal's illness and figure out the absolute best way to address it. Nonetheless, veterinarians are encouraged to stay mindful of any given client's financial concerns and, when possible, start with the least complicated and invasive measures.

Angell's cardiology department was paid tribute in a 2005 *Los Angeles Times* article by nationally syndicated health columnist Judy Foreman, who praised not just the compassionate treatment of her dying cat, but the way the staff took care of her needs as well, allaying her anxiety with frequent updates and reassurance. She wrote,

> His cardiologist, Dr. Nancy Laste, began giving him oxygen, antibiotics and diuretics. Day after day, he hung in, and so did she. Virtually every day for a week, Laste would call me around 9 A.M. and again at 5 P.M. Other staffers telephoned with updates too. I could also call anytime and have someone read me the latest notes on the computer. The hospital and its staff saved my cat's life, but the experience has left me wondering: If an animal hospital can do so well at keeping family members in the loop, why can't people hospitals?

With future plans to expand over the two hospitals to four staff doctors, three cardiology residents, four cardiology technicians, and a secretary, Angell's veterinary cardiology service will be the most extensive in New England. If Laste has anything to say about it, it will also continue to be one of the most compassionate.

Touching a Nerve: Neurology

For nine years, Maureen and Ed Grove's Rosie was a healthy, outgoing dog. A strong, sweet-natured Golden Retriever, she was bright, funny, and so eager on the leash she could practically pull her owners off their feet. Yet when Maureen's ninety-year-old mother or a small neighborhood child was on the other end of the leash, Rosie was the epitome of good canine manners.

When Rosie began having seizures at the age of nine and a half, the Groves took Rosie to Angell to see neurologist Dr. Allen Sisson. An MRI

Dr. Nancy Laste, veterinary cardiologist and Director of Medical Services, Angell Animal Medical Center

scan revealed that Rosie had a tumor (a meningioma) on the left side of her brain. For almost two months, the seizures were managed medically, but when it became clear that medication wasn't helping as much as everyone had hoped, Sisson surgically removed the tumor.

Rosie recovered well from surgery and had only a few subsequent seizures, all far less severe than before the operation. Soon, Rosie was basically back to her old self. Oddly enough, however, six months later, Ed Grove developed the exact same type of tumor his dog had. His meningioma was also successfully treated, and he fully recovered. Grove said, "I figure somebody up there saw how we had treated Rosie."

Sisson adds, "Ed told me jokingly that he wished I could have consulted with his doctors about his surgery too."

Dr. Allen Sisson, veterinary neurologist

Over time, Rosie continued to be monitored at Angell, and a repeat MRI scan of her brain six and a half months post-surgery showed that the tumor was still gone with no sign of growing back. For the next nine months, Rosie was a happy, active dog who gave her owners endless delight. The typical life span for Golden Retrievers is roughly ten to twelve years. Rosie ultimately died peacefully in her sleep at the age of eleven.

Like many of Sisson's clients, Grove and his wife wrote to the neurosurgeon shortly after Rosie's death to express their gratitude for his dedicated care of their beloved family member.

Dear Dr. Sisson,

We want to let you know just how much we've appreciated your treatment of Rosie.

When we first came to you with Rosie's seizure problems, I remember the physical exam you gave her, and I said, "Rosie, it looks like you're getting a very nice massage," because that was how it looked to me. I remember how after we got home, you kept calling us, asking how Rosie was, trying to assess how her condition was and determine how best to continue treating her. I've always, always really felt like you were doing everything you could to help Rosie.

Through your interventions, I'm convinced that you gave us an extra fifteen to sixteen months with Rosie that we wouldn't have had otherwise. I appreciated seeing her in her "little old lady" days. During that time, we developed new bonds with her. It really is true that caring for (or taking care of) someone you love is a privilege. Of course, it was so easy to love her. I can't think of any person in the world (not even my most beloved sister whom I love dearly) who was sweeter than Rosie. There'll never be another like her. She was our companion, sharing our lives . . .

It's a letter Sisson holds dear, as he believes letters like these "express more than anything else why Angell Animal Medical Center exists and what our purpose is—to help kind people and their wonderful pets like these at their time of need to continue to lead happy lives as long as they can, and to know when it is time to say good-bye with dignity."

Rosie was just one of thousands of dogs and cats Sisson has treated since beginning as an intern at Angell in 1979. He has become such an expert in his field that veterinarians around the country have sought consults or flown patients in for physical examinations. "Neurological problems in pets are as common as they are in people and just as treatable," says Sisson. "The exact same percentage of dogs have epilepsy as do humans, and the same percentage can be controlled with medication and are resistant to medical therapy as in people. Dogs develop brain tumors and spinal problems very similar to those in humans."

Angell was one of the first veterinary hospitals in the world to have a veterinarian specializing in neurology on staff, starting in 1969 with the hire of Dr. Damon R. (Skip) Averill, one of the founding members of the American College of Veterinary Internal Medicine. In the 1970s and '80s, the field took off. Just as with human medicine, the advent of first the Computed Tomography (CT) scanner in the 1970s and the Magnetic Resonance Imaging (MRI) scanner the following decade revolutionized veterinary neurology. "For the first time the inside of the brain and spinal cord could be seen in a noninvasive way in a live patient," Sisson explains. "That has made surgical and medical treatment for brain and spinal cord disorders much better."

Over the decades, Angell has obtained the same modern diagnostic and therapeutic equipment used in human medicine to make treatments less invasive and more effective. The service's state-of-the-art diagnostic equipment includes a high-resolution MRI unit that can detect small, subtle lesions and enable intervention early in the disease process. The machine also scans patients in about half the time as earlier equipment, reducing the amount of time an animal is under anesthesia.

Two full-time neurologists diagnose and treat all types of disorders affecting the nervous system. In addition to seizure disorders, the service treats spinal cord disorders, inflammation of the nervous system (such as encephalitis and meningitis), and peripheral nerve and muscle disorders. Surgery can remove brain and spinal tumors, resolve paralysis caused by intervertebral disc herniation, and stabilize spinal instability disorders. And keeping comfort in mind, Angell neurologists work closely with the hospital's Pain Management Services.

The advanced care Angell's neurology department is providing in the twenty-first century affords beloved pets not just a higher quality of life, but more time with the people who love them. Sisson says, "I think the future of veterinary and human neurology is very bright indeed. In recent years, both human and veterinary researchers have begun to fully understand and map the human, canine, and feline genome. Several of the genes that cause inherited, degenerative diseases of the nervous system in humans and animals have recently been identified, helping explain why they cause disease. I believe in the near future there may be effective treatments for some of these devastating degenerative neurological diseases, from Alzheimer's disease in humans to degenerative myelopathy in dogs."

Fighting Feline Diseases: Female Veterinarian Pioneers

Women have had a premier presence in the MSPCA since its earliest days. When George T. Angell founded the MSPCA in 1868, there was someone standing beside him. Emily Appleton, an influential member of Boston society, was one of the first to call on Angell the very morning his provocative letter appeared in the Boston *Daily Advertiser* pleading for all compassionate citizens to join together to stop cruelty to animals. In his work *Autobiography*, Angell writes that to Emily Appleton "more than any other lady in Massachusetts, is the success of our Society due." Although it was deemed improper in 1868 to name a woman as a director of an organization, by 1871 public opinion had changed enough that Emily Appleton was unanimously elected as the first "lady director" of the MSPCA. The MSPCA now bestows an award named after her to an individual who most closely exemplifies the conviction, dedication, and generosity that Mrs. Appleton exhibited.

Two more extraordinary women pioneered some of the era's most groundbreaking work in feline veterinary care. Dr. Jean Holzworth specialized in caring for cats at the hospital from 1950 to 1986. Dr. Susan Cotter came to Angell as an intern in 1966 and stayed on the clinical staff until she went to Tufts University in 1981 to help set up the small animal hospital and create the curriculum for the veterinary school. While women far outnumber men at Angell now, as interns, veterinarians, and in leadership positions, these two were among the few female veterinarians anywhere at the time, itself a groundbreaking accomplishment.

Holzworth turned to veterinary medicine after one of her own beloved cats died from panleukopenia in 1943, before a vaccine for the disease had been developed. "I think Jean was the first ever feline specialist, at least the first woman," Cotter maintains. "She was adamant that cats are not small dogs and need to be treated differently and was a very strong proponent of cats."

"We knew her as Auntie Jean," says Angell surgeon Dr. Mike Pavletic, who worked with Holzworth when he was an intern and resident. (Pavletic purchased Holzworth's house in Hopkinton when she retired, a house fondly recalled as the site of many intern graduation parties.) "She graduated from Cornell at a time when few women were in the profession and was the first to focus on diseases of cats at a time when cats were not nearly as popular as dogs. But she was also an intellectual. She could read and write Latin and Greek fluently, and I think she taught as well before going to vet school."

"She had a very strong personality," Cotter adds. "She could hold her own."

Holzworth and future MSPCA president Dr. Gus Thornton were the first to formally document cases of hyperthyroidism in cats. The most common feline glandular disorder, it was a long-observed condition, but

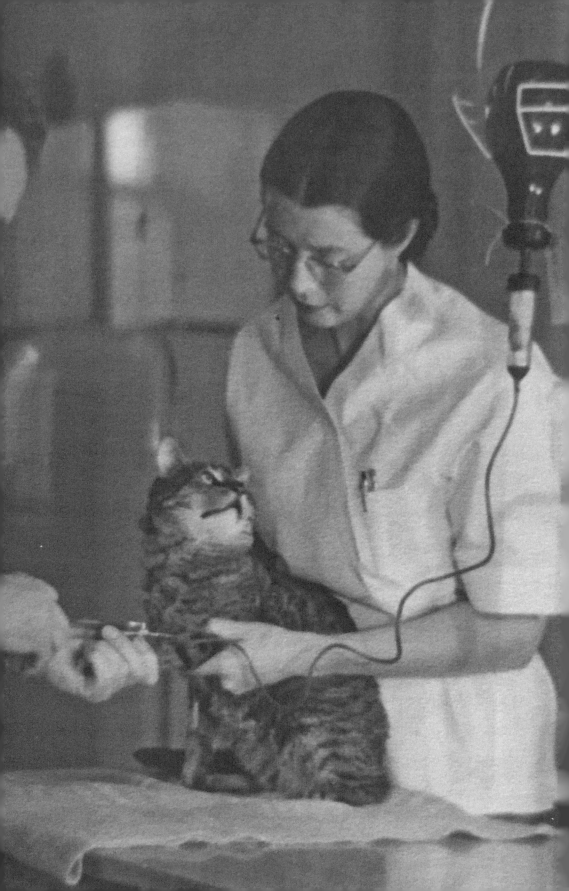

little had been written about it until 1980, when Angell became the first hospital to delineate and disperse information on its complexities. "Jean published the first paper on it," Cotter says "and she published very early papers on leukemia and other blood diseases of cats. She diagnosed trichinosis in her own cat and wrote the first case report on that."

Holzworth also wrote the first book on feline medicine and surgery, the insightful and instructive *Diseases of the Cat: Medicine and Surgery* (W. B. Saunders Co., 1986). The book allowed Holzworth to further share her vast knowledge with pet owners and veterinarians alike. "She would just dig and dig in complicated cases and come up with things that others would overlook," Cotter attests "She had persistence in pursuing unknowns."

Holzworth also had a penchant for clarity and detail, and she was a stickler for correct grammar, often correcting others' medical notes. "One time she talked for a whole hour on misplaced modifiers," Cotter remembers with a laugh. "It was actually fascinating."

Cotter also recalls Holzworth's love of art and opera. When Cotter first came to Boston from Illinois for her Angell internship, she walked into the hospital after driving for two days straight. "I was introduced to Jean, and she said, 'There's a new exhibit at the art museum. We simply must go.'" Cotter overcame her fatigue and off they went, the beginning of a beautiful friendship.

Cotter began her own tenure at Angell as an internist for both dogs and cats. However, in 1970, one very special pet owner changed the direction of her life—an elderly woman named Mary Gravell, who had little money but a big heart and a fierce love for her thirty-seven cats.

Cotter remembers, "She would take in stray cats and people knew that, and cats just found their way to her. Any money she had she spent on them, not on herself. She would come to Angell and was fairly demanding, but she was smart and wanted the best care. However, she couldn't really afford it, and that combination didn't always go over very well, but we sort of bonded."

Then, one by one, Gravell's cats started developing leukemia. At the time, feline leukemia was thought to be a virus transmitted from mother to offspring, so it was unusual to see a spate of the illness in unrelated cats.

Dr. Jean Holzworth, feline veterinary specialist

Across the river in Cambridge, Harvard virologist Max Essex was exploring human retrovirus and thought that cats could offer a good model for study.

Through a mutual friend, Cotter and Essex connected and a plan was hatched. Cotter could do the clinical work of treating Gravell's cats, while Essex could do the follow-up lab research at Harvard, and they would use grant funding to cover Gravell's extensive veterinary bills. "There was no vaccine at the time, so we had no ethical dilemma," Cotter explains. "The only thing we could do was isolate the positive cats and treat them, which Mrs. Gravell hadn't been able to afford to do, so it was mutually beneficial."

For the next seven years, Cotter and Essex went to Gravell's one-room apartment every three months to study feline leukemia in her cats. They discovered the disease was not a virus, but a retrovirus transmitted not just genetically but through saliva as well. Through the study, Cotter and Essex also learned that feline leukemia caused immunodeficiency and bone marrow failure, findings that had profound implications for human AIDS research.

"Max was among the first to think that AIDS was caused by a retrovirus," Cotter says. While there is still no cure for feline leukemia, advanced diagnostic tools and a vaccination to prevent the disease are now standard protocol, developments clearly linked to Cotter's extraordinary dedication to feline health and her groundbreaking work with Gravell's cats.

Treatment at Angell for feline hyperthyroidism has also advanced significantly. Dr. Jean Duddy, who has been at Angell since 1988 and sees both dogs and cats on a daily basis for general medicine and geriatrics, has become Angell's resident expert on feline endocrinology, taking up Holzworth's commitment to understanding and treating hyperthyroidism, as well as diabetes, and parathyroid diseases. Duddy heads a special program called I-131, which uses a radioactive iodine treatment for cats battling hyperthyroidism. Angell was one of the first hospitals in the nation to incorporate the I-131 program, and it is the only one in the Boston area that accepts cats with major medical issues that might complicate the treatment. Currently, the program's success rate is at roughly 97 percent.

In addition, it is the only program that scans all cats first for tumors to verify the most effective form of treatment to prevent unnecessary radiation. The nuclear medicine program also incorporates diagnosis and treatment of seizure disorders, disc disease, vertebral malformations/ instability, and all types of central and peripheral nervous system diseases. And in 2014, the program was given a newly renovated space befitting the extraordinary work taking place for ailing cats.

Healing and Hope: Oncology/Cancer Care Services

Companion animals are susceptible to many of the same kinds of cancer as humans, and cancer is one of the leading causes of death in older pets. But over the past two-plus decades, cancer in pets has become more and more treatable. Chemotherapy and radiation therapy often can give pets and their owners months, even years, longer to cherish their unique relationships.

Take Charlie, a ten-year-old Springer Spaniel diagnosed with a sinonasal carcinoma that spread to his lymph node. He was plagued with frequent sneezing and nasal discharge, and his face was tender and swollen from the tumor, all of which were making the dog feel pretty miserable. While Charlie's cancer was incurable, there was still a lot of life in the affectionate dog, and his owners—and Angell—weren't about to give up on him.

The Angell team started Charlie on palliative radiation to his tumor and lymph node. "Palliative radiation is not curative in intent," explains Angell oncologist Dr. Lyndsay Kubicek, who is one of less than one hundred boarded radiation oncologists in the country. "The goal is to decrease pain and clinical signs associated with the tumor. During radiation we could see the swelling decrease, and Charlie started feeling great. His lymph node also shrunk down to normal size."

Four months out from his diagnosis, Charlie is undergoing chemotherapy treatment with Dr. Ivan Martinez to slow down or possibly prevent the tumor from further progressing. "He has done very well," says Kubicek. "Without the radiation and chemotherapy he would not still be here with us. His quality of life is great."

Charlie's owners agree, and they are thrilled that their beloved dog does not seem to be in any pain. Christopher Vaughn-Martel says, "I still have the picture I took of him right before New Year's Eve with a droopy eye and swollen forehead right before I rushed him to the hospital. I never thought we'd be where we are now with him. Charlie is happy and hungry

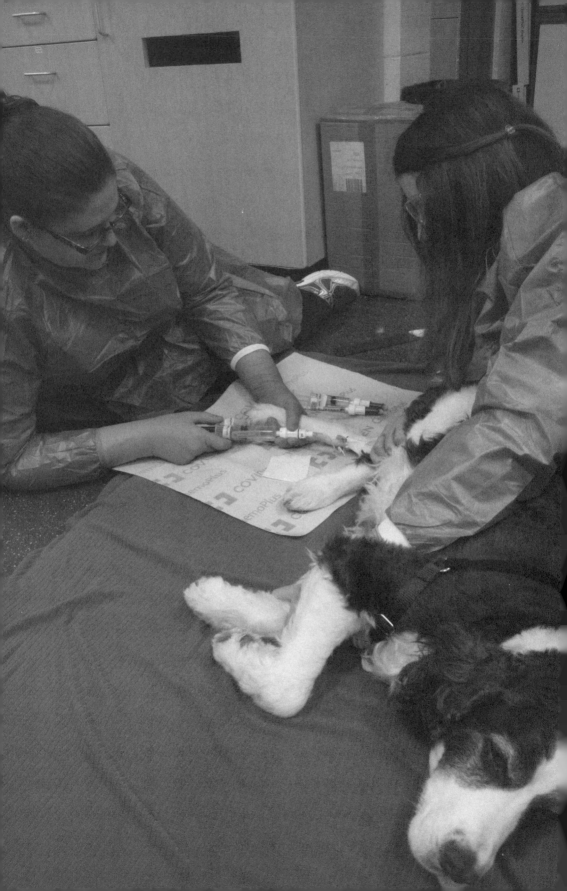

and playful and snuggly and is doing better than I would have guessed possible."

Brian R. Vaughn Martel adds, "The care he (and we!) have received from Angell has been exemplary."

Oncology has been part of Angell's arsenal of care for many years. The hospital established a dedicated Cancer Care Center in 1997, featuring the capacity for onsite radiation therapy. Currently led by oncologists Kubicek and Martinez, it is a small but growing practice that also includes two oncology-dedicated technicians, a board-certified radiation therapist, an oncology assistant, an oncology attendant, an oncology secretary, and a care coordinator assigned to be a facilitator and communication liaison with pet owners through every step of their animal's treatment.

The Center is fully state-of-the-art, using a multidisciplinary approach to cancer diagnosis and treatment, which can include chemotherapy, immunotherapy, and radiation therapy as well as surgery. In-house imaging and pathology services give the Center almost immediate access to many diagnostic tests, and Angell's oncologists work closely with the hospital's surgeons to determine the most appropriate and effective treatment measures for each individual patient. This multimodality approach mirrors the collaborative efforts found in human medicine, and in fact, Angell uses the same advanced technology as many of Boston's top human hospitals.

Angell is one of the few veterinary cancer centers in New England that routinely uses Vascular Access Ports to more comfortably administer treatment without repeated injections. And Angell currently is one of a few veterinary hospitals in New England offering Intensity-Modulated Radiation Therapy (IMRT), which dramatically minimizes side effects by sculpting the radiation treatment beam to the exact size and dimensions of the tumor, helping protect surrounding structures and tissues during treatment. The service also plans to incorporate Stereotactic therapy, or Stereotactic Radiosurgery (SRS). With this advanced technology, very high doses of radiation are delivered to the site of the tumor using a precise beam, allowing for fewer treatment sessions (three or four instead of eighteen to twenty) and making overall treatment less risky.

Charlie receiving his chemotherapy treatments

Unique to Angell is the Center's collaboration with the hospital's Anesthesia and Pain Medicine services to make suffering animals as comfortable and safe as possible. The program can tailor individual pain treatment plans for each animal using novel drug therapies as well as non-drug treatment modalities, such as acupuncture and mobility exercises. "I'm big into proactive pain control," says Kubicek. "We want to prevent pain before it starts. It's important that the pet is comfortable throughout the therapy."

"Our overall goal as veterinary oncologists is to serve our patients, our clients, and continue to work with the human oncology side to find a cure for cancer," says Kubicek. She likes to paraphrase a section from *Small Animal Clinical Oncology*, her field's primary textbook, by Withrow and MacEwen.

> Although our prime directive is to ensure the health and quality of life of the companions under our care, the needs of our client caregivers during the difficult times of cancer diagnosis, treatment and outcome should be of nearly equal importance. Because cancer is a disease that knows no species boundaries, our profession has considerable opportunity to play a key role in comparative oncologic investigations, with the ultimate goal of effecting cure or, in the absence of a cure, transforming cancer from an acute life-threatening disorder into a manageable chronic condition.

The Tooth Hurts: Dentistry Services

When Angell dentist Dr. William Rosenblad first met Fritz, a seven-year-old Miniature Schnauzer, the adorable, energetic little dog was the picture of health from all outward appearances. While another veterinarian had already done some basic dental work on Fritz, including a couple of extractions, the dog was referred to Rosenblad to remove a few additional loose teeth.

However, after Rosenblad examined Fritz and took X-rays of the dog's mouth, he discovered not just a few wiggly teeth, but massive periodontal disease. Rosenblad ended up having to extract more than thirty of the dog's teeth. Rosenblad explains, "Without proper treatment, he would have lost all of his teeth over time, with much pain, and possibly even jaw fracture(s) due to bone loss from the periodontal disease and abscessed teeth. After I showed Fritz's owner the extent of the disease on the radiographs, he

Dr. William Rosenblad, head of Dentistry services

thanked me profusely. But he was horrified at the veterinary profession, that even though he brushed his dog's teeth every day, no one had told him to see me sooner about the loose teeth, to start thinking about abscesses and better preventive care. He ended up writing the American Veterinary Medicine Association to implore them to get veterinary colleges to do more dental education. That made my day."

In fact, Rosenblad is a man on a mission to get veterinarians and pet owners alike better educated about the importance of pet oral hygiene and to spread the word about the prevalence of periodontal disease, which is the single most common disease in pet cats and dogs. It affects 85 percent of dogs and cats over the age of two, though Rosenblad says he has seen many pets develop issues while only months old. Since starting the hospital's Dentistry service in 1998, he and his team have developed it into one of only three full-time veterinary specialty dentistry services in New England. In 2014, they performed more than 850 surgeries.

Rosenblad believes that the high rate of dental issues in pets is largely due to lack of awareness, not just by owners but by veterinarians as well. "There's a lack of teaching dentistry in most veterinary schools. Even proper oral exams are not taught well. Only a third of the schools in the country have full-time dentistry departments. Go back to the nineties, and there were only three in total. It's an aspect of medicine that's very under-served by the profession, so if vets don't notice dental disease, how are owners supposed to?"

As with people, dental issues can result in tremendous discomfort for animals. But since an animal's survival instinct is to mask pain, its owner may not perceive a problem. Rosenblad explains that much of the time "doggie breath" is often an infection, and fighting the pain of chronic infection can be a huge drain on an animal's energy as well as its immune system. He has seen animals transformed by a simple tooth extraction. "Owners have told me their pets show a whole new level of energy, appe-tite, interest in grooming."

Rosenblad says that part of what makes his service unique in the vet-erinary world is not just his own expertise, but also the fact that over the years he has managed to get his Angell colleagues to increase their knowl-edge and commitment as well. "I've got everyone looking in mouths, and Angell's entire staff recognizes dental disease and the importance of how it fits into the whole health of an animal," he says. "Every single specialty here has referred patients to me."

In addition to cleanings and extractions, Angell's advanced dental pro-cedures include root canals, orthodontics, tumor resections, and jaw frac-tures involving teeth. Roughly half of Rosenblad's patients are referred by other veterinary practices, and a significant number come to Angell through emergencies. One of Rosenblad's most well-known cases involved a one-year-old Terrier named Jack, who was kicked in the face by a 2,200-pound horse. He had such a severe combination of jaw and tooth trauma that Rosenblad was surprised the dog had survived the accident. "When he got here, he had shattered teeth and jaw pieces, and I had to put everything back together. But literally, the next day after surgery, you could not tell.

He looked normal from the outside and was happy and functional. He did great."

Because Rosenblad works so closely with other specialists, he and his team are renowned for being able to work skillfully as well as efficiently on patients who have other clinical issues that can make anesthesia more tricky. He thinks fear of anesthesia is what keeps many owners from pursuing better dental care for their pets. "There's a lot of misinformation, and the protocols in dentistry used to be terrible. Everybody here has a nightmare story. But now it's much better, and to quote my colleague cardiologist Dr. [Nancy] Laste, we fear the progression of dental disease much more than properly performed anesthesia."

Rosenblad takes every opportunity he can to share his knowledge and expertise with vet students, interns, and residents at Angell. "I often work in concert with residents to guide them through jaw fracture repairs, tumor resections, so that they're prepared to do that if and when they go to practice somewhere that doesn't have dental services, which is most places."

Equally important for Rosenblad is educating clients, not just showing them the hows and whys of a needed procedure, but advocating for preventive care. "Nothing beats daily tooth brushing. It's like flossing for humans. The problem is, people aren't often taught to brush their pet's teeth properly, and by the time I see them, dental disease has already taken hold. I'm trying to educate vets and clients that you can never start too soon with brushing and cleaning. If you don't do it early, pets will develop disease, and then it will be painful for them to have their teeth brushed. My colleagues do a great job talking to pet owners about this, too, and the client response has been tremendous. I have some owners bringing me their third and fourth generation of pets."

The Multiplicity of the Species: Avian and Exotic Medicine

On any given day, most vets deal with a varied collection of cats and dogs. But for Angell's Dr. Elisabeth Simone-Freilicher, who works in Angell's two-decade-old Avian and Exotics department, nearly every appointment is with a different species. She might have a chinchilla with dental problems followed by an egg-bound budgie followed by an elderly rabbit with arthritis. She recently had back-to-back bleeders—a ferret bleeding from

its belly and an axolotl (a kind of salamander) bleeding from the gills. The week before, she had a run on neurological issues. "I had a rat with a pituitary tumor and a bird that was picking at its foot, which seemed more medical than behavioral," she recalls. Blood tests ensued, and a medication was found that treated both neurological possibilities and arthritis.

There are fewer than 140 avian specialists in the world, but Angell has two of them: Dr. Simone-Freilicher and Dr. Brendan Noonan, both senior clinicians. Both veterinarians offer wellness care as well as emergency and critical care services for birds and exotic pets, from small mammals to reptiles and fish. Simone-Freilicher completed additional specialty training in exotic medicine, including rabbit and rodent dentistry, medical and surgical treatment of ferret diseases, and reptile medicine and surgery. The department has state-of-the-art equipment and facilities specially designed for the wide range of species that walk through Angell's doors. The department has also developed specialized diagnostic and treatment protocols. Even so, some of the medical issues and treatment options the veterinarians confront are not always in the books.

"We don't have the studies, so some of the drug treatments can be hit or miss," Simone-Freilicher says. "The species are so different, you can't always extrapolate that what works for one will help another. An Amazon parrot versus a cockatiel is like the difference between a cow and a rabbit."

Simone-Freilicher has had a special fondness for birds since childhood, and she was only five years old when she told her parents she wanted to be a vet. But by college, she had developed an interest in ecology. As an ecology major undergraduate at North Carolina State, she was part of a team of researchers working with the veterinary school's wildlife service. When the service found a red tail hawk that needed physical therapy for rehab, Simone-Freilicher jumped at the opportunity and began to realize that her interest in the medical issues of animal welfare outshone her appetite for ecology, so she decided to go to veterinary school and specialize in caring for birds. She remembers reading the first avian medical textbook ever written, *Diseases of Cage and Aviary Birds* (1969) by long-time Angell clinician Dr. Margaret Petrak. The landmark book is still used by veterinary students today, and Simone-Freilicher recalls reading it cover

Dr. Elisabeth Simone-Freilicher, Avian and Exotics Specialist to cover, with "stars in my eyes, never dreaming I'd be here practicing!" (Later in her career, "Midge" Petrak, one of the many remarkable Angell women in the hospital's history, became a commissioned MSPCA Law Enforcement officer.)

With Petrak's efforts in avian care laying the groundwork, Angell officially established a specialty service in Avian and Exotics Medicine in 1994. Simone-Freilicher says the most challenging aspect of the department's work is the delicacy of most of the patients. "That and the fact that they hide their illness so that the owners don't know they're sick until they are in really desperate shape. Yet in diagnosing and treating, you have to be very careful to do everything slowly and in stages because you can put them over the edge if you do too much. But it's so rewarding when you navigate that dance well and something that came here in really desperate shape gets better and goes home."

She remembers a budgie that was sucked into a shop vac who survived to tell the tale following a partial amputation of its wing. There was another bird treated for tuberculosis, and an iguana with bad arthritis whose quality of life was improved by acupuncture.

The connection is the human factor. "What people outside the field don't understand is how important these pets can be to people," Simone-Freilicher maintains. Even those with short life spans can engender strong bonds. From her early days practicing in New York, she recalls a woman who once brought in an ailing hamster. "He was really sick, so we did ultrasound and blood work, with this adult woman begging us not to let her hamster die. With fluid injections, the hamster was given another good six months, and I remember her coming in and thanking us so profusely, it almost seemed over the top."

Simone-Freilicher later realized that the woman had been recently bereaved and put it together with the fact that it was not long after 9/11. She concludes, "This little pet might have been all she had."

Often times with birds and exotics, it's children who push for care, to the consternation of parents. "People sometimes think if you only spent ten dollars to buy a pet, why spend five hundred dollars to get him well?" she says, acknowledging that sometimes those decisions can be tremendously fraught, especially for families of limited income. But she refuses to entertain the occasional parent's suggestion of subterfuge to spare a child's pain, such as replacing a failing parakeet or guinea pig with another newly bought lookalike under the guise that the animal got well.

"Children know if they're very attached that you've replaced one animal for another one, and it sets up a subconscious trust issue with parents. You just have to say, 'Look, this is hard, but it's time to have the conversation about dealing with death.' And I tell them there is no reason you have to go forward with treatment if you can't afford it. That's an important lesson too. But as a parent, you have to value what your kids value."

And like all veterinarians, she must embody a little bit of the psychologist in helping owners deal with grief. She adds, "People can be every bit as attached to an exotic pet as they are to their dogs and cats."

Layers of Support: Angell's Nurses and Technicians

One of the most important advancements at Angell in the 1980s and '90s was the elevation of the hospital's technical support and nursing staff, who can perform many of the functions previously restricted to veterinarians, such as drawing blood samples, inserting intravenous catheters, and performing electrocardiograms. While the hospital's doctors may get the bulk of the glory, most of them are quick to credit Angell's support staff with enabling them to do what they do so effectively. Often the hospital's unsung heroes, the support staff provide skilled, efficient, and compassionate care directly to patients, although often from behind the scenes.

Dr. Michael Pavletic, Angell's Director of Surgery services, maintains, "The nurses, anesthesia technicians, and surgical staff are vital to day-to-day operations. This includes our anesthesiologists, who also oversee the most critical surgical cases."

Angell's Anesthesia service, led by Dr. Ashley Barton-Lamb and Dr. Stephanie Krein, is considered one of the hospital's most vital specialties, heavily relied upon for ensuring the safest and most effective anesthesia protocols. Specially trained veterinary technicians are critical to the service, monitoring patients for blood pressure, carbon dioxide, oxygen, and heart rate during procedures ranging from routine sedation for radiographs to general anesthesia for surgery.

As Angell has incorporated more specialty medicine over the decades, the role of veterinary technicians and nurses has become increasingly specialized as well, with staff becoming more highly trained for the specific needs of all the hospital's many services. Senior surgery technician Rose Henle, who has worked at Angell for a remarkable forty-six years, says that in the early days, there was less distinction between nurses and technicians, both of whom were more free to go where needed to handle a variety of tasks, which is still the model in many small veterinary practices. Training was often a kind of "baptism by fire." She explains, "When I started out, technicians didn't have to be certified. They were trained by doctors and other individuals in the department and learned by experience."

However, with more specialized knowledge required for sophisticated procedures and equipment, technicians now undergo a strict certification process. Henle says, "I've seen Angell [grow] from a small place on Longwood Avenue that was very personal, almost like a family." She adds, "Patient care has become much better. People are much better trained, and there is much better equipment to know how a patient is doing."

Angell nurse Joan Fontaine, who has worked at the hospital since 1979, agrees. "Angell has seen a lot of changes. The structural changes are almost a constant. The medicine changes as well. Veterinary medicine is not as evidence-based as is human medicine, especially in the teaching hospitals, but you will see constant practice changes. Angell does strive to be at the forefront of solid medical techniques, something that seems to be delayed or lacking altogether in small practices."

Fontaine believes it is often the nurses who are able to track the holistic view of a patient, which she says can sometimes get lost in the mechanics of doing a procedure. "I never had a desire to become a veterinarian," says Fontaine, who has worked in human medicine as well, becoming an EMT while studying wildlife biology in college. "I wanted the challenge of directly working with the patients, something that becomes less of an opportunity if you became a DVM. I hear people say they want to become a veterinarian because they don't like people, but they fail to realize you are spending a majority of your time with the clients, not with the patients."

With nurses, techs, and doctors all working together toward common goals, Angell benefits from a multilayered synergy to care fueled by a shared mission and sense of camaraderie. While this approach provides

Senior surgery technician Rose Henle

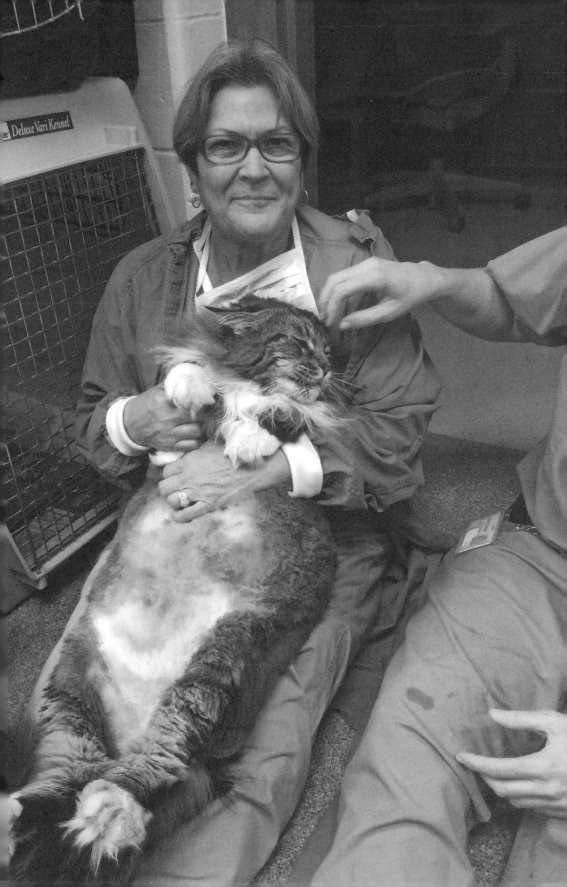

appropriate checks and balances, it's not surprising that there's sometimes a little head-butting along the way, a dynamic perhaps not unlike that in human medicine. Emergency and Critical Care Director Kiko Bracker says, "A lot of the nurses have been here for decades, and they know what they're doing, and there's a real sense of ownership. It can be a little challenging to have Dr. XYZ come in fresh from med school, and sometimes doctors have a hard time getting used to that. But when we graduate interns and residents, they often get back to us and say they had no idea of the quality of nursing staff while they were here, and now they miss their expertise so much."

Fontaine believes Angell's fast pace and extensive patient load attract a very special breed of caregiver. "Veterinary schools can see something like seven thousand patient visits a year. Angell sees sixty-thousand-plus a year. From veterinary interns to the nursing and tech staff, it can be difficult to function at that pace. The people who thrive in that environment are few, and many people moving from a small practice to Angell can be overwhelmed."

She says that the pace, diversity, and commitment are part of what keep her at Angell. "I could never switch to a small practice. I have found that the core people we work with stay in their positions because they care about doing their best for the patients. We all work cooperatively to ensure the best outcome for our patients. People who aren't there for that reason usually don't last long. I think everyone works very hard to get the best outcome for every patient that comes to Angell; otherwise the long, hard hours that we all put in 24-7 would be not worth it. That is why we are here every day."

PART THREE

ANGELL IN
THE TWENTY-FIRST CENTURY

"MY WIFE always said it didn't count as work because I looked forward to it every single day," says Dr. Peter Theran of his forty-two years at Angell. "What a wonderful place to spend my entire veterinary career. By the time I retired in 2003, I felt like I'd started in the Dark Ages and come through this huge transformation."

In 2001, the MSPCA–Angell launched a multimillion-dollar campaign for a major renovation of the facility, designed to improve the MSPCA adoption services as well as greatly expand Angell's capacity for taking care of ailing animals. When veterinarian Dr. Larry M. Hawk became president of the MSPCA in 2003, he felt new branding was in order. Hawk realigned the organization to better coordinate and showcase the depth of its humane and veterinary services. Under the new name MSPCA–Angell, the organization began referring to its animal shelters as animal care and adoption centers, and the flagship veterinary hospital in Boston was renamed Angell Animal Medical Center. A marketing plan that included a new website (www.mspca.org) was put in place, and George T. Angell's groundbreaking publication, *Our Dumb Animals* (renamed *Animals* in 1972), was transformed into *Companion*, a full-color newsletter published twice a year.

The MSPCA established the Angell Animal Poison Control hotline, available 24-7 to pet owners and veterinarians for consultation with experts in veterinary toxicology. In 2003, the hospital installed a new MRI designed specifically for imaging animals—the first in New England and only the second available in the country. (Now the hospital has a state-of-the-art human MRI with increased speed and resolution.) The following year, construction began on an MRI suite as part of the building campaign to expand veterinary and adoption services.

In 2010, Chairman of the Board Robert Cummings, Esq., retired after having served on the Board since 1966 in numerous capacities. Hillery Ballantyne was elected, the first woman to serve in this capacity. The American Humane Education Society (AHES) and the Center for Laboratory Animal Welfare (CLAW) were merged into the MSPCA.

Carter Luke, President and CEO of the MSPCA–Angell and his dog, Teddy

CHAPTER 7

Carter Luke and Angell's Expansion

IN MAY OF 2006, Carter Luke was appointed President and CEO of the MSPCA–Angell. He was formerly the MSPCA's Executive Vice President and Vice President for Animal Protection. Luke, as he prefers to be called, began his professional life as an elementary school teacher in Wisconsin before becoming shelter manager of Coulee Region Humane Society in LaCrosse. Before joining the MSPCA in 1985, he was an executive director of the Dane County Humane Society in Madison. He is a founding board member of both the National Council on Pet Population Study and Policy and the Massachusetts Animal Coalition, and is a member of the Hoarding of Animals Research Consortium. For more than twenty years, he has been extensively involved in research areas such as pet-population dynamics, free-roaming cats, cruelty and violence toward animals, dangerous dogs, and animal hoarding. He has published widely on issues relating to the interaction between humans and animals, including exploring the roots of violence directed toward animals.

After taking over as President of the MSPCA, Luke began reinforcing the organization's mission for compassionate care. "What really counts about how Angell operates is the way each animal comes through our doors one at a time," he claims. "Each is an individual, with a name. (For those who come to us as lost or abandoned, we give them a name.) Each case is a little different, but it is personal, not institutional. Like so many others who place their trust in our Angell team when their furry family members are most vulnerable, I am a client here, too. As President, I track the numbers, but when I am sitting across an exam table from our veterinarian, I'm worried about Teddy or Scoots or Lunar or Gilligan."

In June of 2006, just a month after Luke's appointment, the MSPCA–Angell unveiled the newly expanded facility at 350 South Huntington.

The fundraising campaign launched in 2001 raised more than $16 million dollars entirely from donations, ranging from generous contributions by major donors to small, personal offerings by grateful pet owners. Luke calls it "a beautiful dream come true." The new addition to the medical center, named the Helen Schmidt Stanton Clinical Care Center, expanded hospital space by almost twenty-five thousand square feet and dramatically increased Angell's capabilities to treat and care for more animals than ever before.

With the expansion, the facility's main entrance was flipped to the back. Big double doors lead into the lobby, conveniently adjacent to the large parking lot. In addition to separate waiting areas for different species, the lobby setup includes a separate "Triage Area" for emergency patient intake.

Other specialized examination rooms were created with unique features specific to the needs of Angell's numerous specialties, each with direct access to a centralized Treatment Area. A new Diagnostic Imaging Room was equipped with a portable ultrasound machine, a new MRI, and a digital X-Ray machine to provide immediate results. The pharmacy, previously a small area in the old part of the building, was transformed into a bright spacious area conveniently next to the area for check-out. Client amenities included a children's playroom for restless youngsters and a Family Meditation Room for clients needing a quiet, private setting, such as confronting the possibility of euthanasia for a beloved pet.

Luke reflected on the expansion in *Companion,*

> For thirty years, clients and pets came to us through Angell Animal Medical Center's serviceable but less-than-uplifting entrance, threaded their way through a confusing check-in system, and sat down to wait in a crowded, noisy room. Then on June 19, 2006, everything changed. People and pets walked amazed into the vast and airy lobby of our new Helen Schmidt Stanton Clinical Center, with its emergency triage system, streamlined check-in, and species-specific waiting areas. . . . Our new building symbolizes our renewed energy, our renewed resolve to secure a bright future for our cause.

Today, one of the first things people notice walking through the door of AAMC is a big screen suspended above the front desk area with a slideshow of pets that have been helped at Angell. It's an effective way of setting

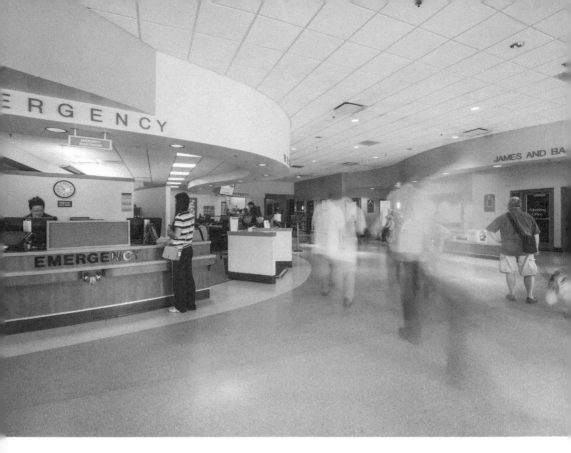

A view of the busy Angell Animal Medical Center lobby today

a tone that makes a big, sophisticated urban medical facility feel as warm and welcoming as a small-town veterinary practice. "People get so excited when they see their pets up there," maintains Mary Grace, Angell's Director of Hospital Operations.

The new construction also traded the former adoption facility, with its dark, cramped atmosphere, for the bright, roomy, and welcoming Copeland Family Animal Care and Adoption Center next to the hospital lobby. The new center is four times larger than the previous space, and adoptions began to skyrocket—especially for cats, since the hospital waiting area for felines had windows into the cat rooms in the adoption center. In August, the center opened the Shalit-Glazer Clinic, which continues to provide spay/neuter services to qualified low-income pet owners for a nominal fee, furthering the MSPCA's mission to address pet overpopulation by reducing the number of unwanted kittens and puppies.

Dr. Lisa Moses with an acupuncture patient

CHAPTER 8

Specialty Services

ONE OF THE BIGGEST draws of Angell in the twenty-first century is the breadth and quality of the hospital's specialty services, which prompt referrals from veterinarians throughout New England and beyond. In 2007, Angell became one of a small group of veterinary schools and practices to offer pain medicine services. Following the example set by human medical practices, the specialty recognized the importance of assessing and treating animal pain with just as sophisticated means.

Sweet Relief: Pain Medicine

On opening day for the Red Sox, heavy traffic has made Kathy Burdon late for her dog Holly's appointment with Dr. Lisa Moses in Angell's Pain Medicine service. Burdon usually likes to arrive early and let her fourteen-year-old Lab walk around a bit and get settled before going in for treatment. But Holly seems surprisingly relaxed, tail wagging, when the warm, soft-spoken Moses welcomes her into the exam room. As Moses' assistant, Sonya Greenberg, plies Holly with Buddy Biscuits, the Lab plops down on the floor, and Moses quickly and gently inserts more than a dozen acupuncture needles into critical spots on the dog's legs, back, and head. Distracted by the cookies, Holly seems quite content. As she settles in, Moses turns down the lights and chats amiably with Burdon.

Burdon has been bringing her beloved dog to the Pain Medicine service for two years for Moses' unique ministrations, which always include a generous dose of compassion and insight. Under Moses' direction, the Pain Medicine service assesses and manages both chronic pain, such as arthritis, and acute pain, like that from surgery and trauma. Individualized treatment plans often combine a variety of modalities, from multiple types of drug therapy, nerve blocks, and other forms of local anesthesia, to acupuncture, trigger point therapy, physical therapy, and lifestyle changes. For Moses, the art and science of relieving animal pain starts with seeing the whole animal. It is a comprehensive approach that takes into consideration all the different medical issues an animal might be struggling with, as well as the expected vicissitudes of aging.

"We want for our pets what we want for people—to have a great quality of life in our elder years," Moses says.

Moses is unique in the veterinary world. Board certified in internal medicine with advanced training in both human and veterinary pain medicine, she was a senior clinician in Angell's Emergency and Critical Care service for twelve years before starting the Pain Medicine service in 2007. Moses' distinctive combination of training and experience enables her to manage complex cases requiring simultaneous treatment of multiple medical issues, and she collaborates closely with Angell's specialists to make sure all aspects of care are complementary and coordinated.

Moses says Holly is one of the relatively easy ones. Acupuncture, NSAIDs (non-steroidal, anti-inflammatory drugs), and physical therapy have successfully addressed the discomfort of the Lab's chronic liver disease and arthritis. "I think she has a nice life," says Moses.

"Holly definitely has a full Rolodex," agrees Burdon with a little laugh. "I don't think she'd still be with us without this. Between the mental and physical stimulation, she acts three to four years younger."

Most of Moses' cases are significantly more complicated. The majority of her patients are not only advanced in age, they are also battling a combination of problems, and chronic pain can be due to a number of conditions. On the exam room wall is a picture of a Border Collie named Maggie, red felt antlers perched rakishly on her head. "When I first saw her, she was paralyzed in the back end from a spinal cord injury, was in a wheelchair, and hadn't walked in six months. They couldn't repair the injury, but she ended up being able to walk in the last two years of her life with a combination of intensive drug and pain management, electro-acupuncture to help stimulate nerve function, and management of incontinence and bladder infections. We addressed the whole picture. She lived to be seventeen and a half."

Moses treats not only dogs and cats, but also any companion animal species—birds, hedgehogs, rabbits, even mice and snakes. She recently treated a thirteen-year-old iguana with bad arthritis and heart failure with acupuncture and drug therapy. "The owner thought my treatment made a big difference in his mobility," Moses says.

She also enabled a fifty-two-year-old Macaw who had been unable to grasp his perch because of bad arthritis to return to his roost again. Arthritis is one of the most common issues Moses treats. "Everything that has a joint can have arthritis," she explains. "Lots of people assume chronic arthritis is simply a fact of life and something that you don't intervene with, but I think that's about as pure a quality of life issue as there is, and if it's making animals isolate themselves or taking away things that give them pleasure, then we should do something about it. I also treat a lot of neurologic diseases common from aging, just like for people."

In fact, the Pain Medicine service is modeled after pain clinics at human hospitals, and the majority of Moses' training in palliative care and pain medicine came from studying human health-care models. She spends time every year at various human hospitals observing practices. Moses makes a clear distinction between palliative care and hospice care, which is about providing end-of-life comfort and support after treatment for a primary disease has been stopped. She describes palliative care as medical treatment focused on improving quality of life for the patient regardless of diagnosis and prognosis. "It's not about patients who have a terminal diagnosis. Palliative care starts from the moment of diagnosis and stands alongside any other kind of treatment and care. Too often, people don't seek palliative care until a pet is really close to the end of life and they've missed out on an opportunity to make their animal feel better much earlier. My patients don't have to be dying for me to make them feel better."

Moses believes some types of pain are under-recognized, such as dental pain, ear infections, skin problems, and eye problems, and she admits that it's not always easy to detect pain in an animal. Sometimes the signs of pain, especially chronic pain, can be subtle, especially in animals prone to mask their vulnerability as an evolutionary survival mechanism. Moses talks to owners about noticing changes in behavior—such as not jumping on a bed anymore, avoiding stairs, losing interest in a favorite toy, or making changes in toileting posture. "I have to assess that pain based on changes in behavior and function, because we don't have other ways to do it. For example, if a dog can't lift its leg to pee because it can't balance, that's a good indicator something's wrong."

First-time clients to the Pain Medicine Service are asked to fill out a long questionnaire that helps Moses get a thorough picture of how a pet previously functioned and what it used to do for pleasure that it can no longer do. She then works with clients to help them identify the top three to five medical issues impacting their pet's function and comfort. This helps her prioritize possible treatment options, trying to balance the needs of both pet and owner. "If an owner can't provide the level of care that's needed without hardship, nobody's going to be helped."

The goal is to see more engagement and energy while enabling the return of behaviors that were normal earlier in life. "For a lot of my patients who are so physically disabled they can't do the kind of things they used to do, we might do nose work classes that are intellectually stimulating but don't require a lot of physical ability. I might also prescribe small amounts of exercise, which is a powerful internal trigger of pain relief."

Moses adds, "I also have been able to start addressing the cognitive emotional component. We know now that the pathways in the brain for pain are the same as for emotion, so when the brain changes in response to pain, it changes cognitive function. We can't ignore that piece of it."

Moses' dream is for true palliative care medicine to become a more distinct part of veterinary medicine, especially regarding training for primary care practitioners. "They have the long-term relationship and are in a really good position to help people decide whether suffering is occurring and what to do about it. They need to have real conversations about chronic pain and end-of-life care, just like with people." She is working at Angell to institute a model in which a pain care consult is part of an initial treatment plan for any diagnosis involving chronic pain.

Given the advanced age of most of Moses' patients, she says she never has a day without a conversation about euthanasia. "Sometimes, it's with all my appointments, and it's agonizing. The clients whom I work with I generally really love, and it's hard to say good-bye. Some of them stay in touch with me for years later, like one woman who regularly sends me a box of dog cookies for my patients, even though her own dog has been gone a long time."

Moses says, "The thing about Angell is that we are truly collaborative. We don't fight over cases. We don't want credit. If someone in the building can do a better job on a piece of the case, we page them from the exam room, and get that person's advice. I think that's why a lot of people like me have been here this long. We're not a business first and foremost. Our reason for being is truly animal-focused care, to give the best care we can for the patient and take care of the people, too. I work here because in every room I go into in the hospital, somebody is on the floor making baby noises at an animal, whether it's in an exam room or an office upstairs. I can't imagine not spending my days with people who share that sense of purpose about what we do."

Creatures of Habit: Behavior Services

While pain can cause some animals to act uncharacteristically, sometimes strange behavior isn't driven by discomfort, but by some other underlying issue. That's where Angell's Behavior services come into play.

When Angell behaviorist Dr. Terri Bright first met Pepper, a young Bull Terrier, the dog was "kind of a train wreck." Bred by a backyard breeder, Pepper had been taken from the litter too early and sold to a pet store, where she was bought by someone who didn't socialize her properly. Pepper grew up fearful and aggressive, and after a year, the owner gave up and turned her in to a breed rescue group.

That's where Bright found Pepper and decided to take on the responsibility of fostering her. Since Pepper was too fearful to be adopted, Bright's husband adored Pepper, and Bright was a burgeoning trainer, they kept her. "I thought I could help her, so I took her to lots of different classes," she recalls.

What Bright discovered through the process was a bit of a revelation. "I found myself getting used to having a fearful, barky, aggressive dog, and realized that was never going to change. What happens in puppyhood stays for life, and she'd had a terrible background."

But while she might not be able to change Pepper's nature, Bright knew she could train alternative responses in the dog's behavior. An alternative response to fearfulness or aggression can be as simple as a "Come, sit, stay" cue, rewarded by a treat. "You can't use words to mediate fear in animals, but you can make things in the environment less frightening by pairing them with opportunities for good things," says Bright.

She elaborates, "Pepper's failure taught me that there's no cure for behavior, which people don't often hear from trainers. It's the same as with those we know who quit drinking or smoking. If that behavior is in their repertoire, there is always a risk of relapsing in the future." To that end, Bright says any training of animals involves training their owners, too, as well as carefully managing the environment of the animal.

Bright began working her magic with other dogs as well. Along the way, she earned her Master of Science degree and PhD at Simmons College in Applied Behavior Analysis (ABA) with an animal specialty, and she became a Board-Certified Behavior Analyst (BCBA-D) and a Certified Applied Animal Behaviorist (CAAB). Since 2007, she has used that rare combination of human and animal behavior expertise in developing the MSPCA–Angell's Behavior services, making the hospital one of only three facilities in New England with a behaviorist on staff.

Bright says animals with behavior problems are usually very bright and responsive to training—even cats, who are known for being very independent. "But the training approach is different; you have to set aside more time," Bright says. "It's a cat-led experience. Cats are not motivated to please people, and when they say the session is over, it's over." But she says that if you create a cat-friendly training environment, you can teach cats to go to a mat, stay in place, and even do agility, which is a sport/training tool that Bright calls "insanely fun" in which animals are trained and rewarded to run a kind of obstacle course. (One of Bright's own dogs, Fanny, was a nationally ranked competitor in the sport.)

She recalls one five-year-old cat whose owner was referred to her by the MSPCA–Angell's Vice President of Development, Alice Bruce. The cat was suffering from psychogenic alopecia—also known as over-grooming—as well as extreme fearfulness. "The cat spent her day hiding, all day, every day. With our help, she learned to do agility. Following our instructions, the owner taught her to follow a target stick over hurdles and through tunnels, and would reward her with cat treats. She loves to do agility, and the change in this cat is wonderful. We use the video of her for other cat owners." Bright also worked with the referring vet and with Angell's Dr. Jean Duddy, who found that the cat had food allergies. When these were addressed, the over-grooming stopped. This cat is now confident, she looks forward to training every day, and all of her hair has grown back.

In 2013, Bright launched Angell's clinical Behavior services to address issues such as fear, aggression, anxiety, separation anxiety, and other concerns, seeing roughly three hundred clinical patients annually. The program is in such demand that appointments are booked three or four months in advance. Assessing each case is an intensive process, resulting in a nearly ten-page behavior plan for each animal. Two training coordinators and a behavior technician help with follow-up appointments. A staff of seven dog trainers also teach the department's thirty-five classes each week to members of the public with their dogs. Cross-referrals are often made between the pet classes and the clinical practice. "The level of service here is extraordinary," Bright maintains. "It's unique in the country."

Behavior services is the only program that bridges both the MSPCA and Angell Animal Medical Center. In addition to clinical appointments, Bright supervises the trainers and works in the shelter, helping staff devise best behavior plans for dogs in the shelter or those having trouble with the

Dr. Terri Bright with two of her Bull Terriers

adoption transition. She also teaches in the SafeWalk program, a nationally known curriculum she developed six years ago to train human volunteers in good practices around shelter dogs. Bright says with pride, "Since we started SafeWalk, we have increased the adoption rates of Pit Bulls from 77 percent to 91 percent, and have a phalanx of amazingly well-trained and devoted volunteers."

For her dissertation, Bright developed a dog behavior assessment and analysis tool to standardize how dog trainers evaluate the cause of problem behaviors. "I use it with every appointment, and I'm working on publishing it so we can roll it out as a workbook to use for teaching trainers. Typically, trainers just modify behavior. But there is a difference between modifying behavior and finding why it happens and using that cause to get the best results."

Bright is unique in applying knowledge gleaned from studies of human behavior modification to her work with animals in a hospital and shelter setting. "It's primarily been done with animals in a few zoos and aquariums, but it's very effective with dogs and cats. The science of Pavlov and Skinner applies across all organisms, humans included. It's all the same science, and changing the behavior of multiple species is a great calling."

Seeing the Light: Ophthalmology

Though veterinary ophthalmology wasn't officially established nationally as a specialty until 1970, it was practiced at Angell more than a decade earlier. Dr. Todd Munson, one of the hospital's most esteemed internal medicine veterinarians, was fascinated by diseases of the eye. In the late 1950s, he began dedicating part of his clinical time to the study and practice of ophthalmology. He was joined a few years later by Dr. Richard Donovan, and the two began expanding services in eye care at Angell. During their tenure, the two veterinarians significantly contributed to advances in surgical techniques, from eyelid abnormalities to cataract removal. They started to recognize and screen for inherited eye defects, documenting their findings to share with the veterinary world at large.

Over the next decades, other notable clinicians carried the flag at Angell for veterinary ophthalmology, including Rhea Morgan and Noelle McNabb. Today, Angell's state-of-the-art ophthalmology department is led by Dr. Daniel Biros and Dr. Martin Coster and provides a wide range of medical and surgical interventions for almost every eye disease. The service handles a diverse, high-volume caseload, not just cats and dogs but exotic pets as well.

Just as with people, one of the most common surgeries the ophthalmologists perform is cataract surgery for sight restoration. But the Angell team also has performed a number of unusual, sometimes life-saving procedures as well. Some of their work involves emergency situations and special referrals by other veterinarians. Several years ago, an eight-year-old German Shorthaired Pointer named Jake plowed into a tree branch during a spirited trek through the woods near his home in South Hamilton and lodged a stick behind his right eye. While a local veterinarian removed the part of the stick lodged between the dog's eyelids, he knew Jake needed the specialized services of a veterinary ophthalmologist and sent him to Angell.

Not so long ago, removal of the eye might have been the obvious choice. However, Coster, along with Angell's Director of Surgery, Dr. Mike Pavletic, performed a delicate two-hour operation that carefully removed the remainder of the stick. The surgery restored not only Jake's sight, but his gregarious spirit as well.

In other cases, Angell ophthalmologists have used innovative techniques, such as with a playful shelter kitten named Phil. The three-month-old kitten was born without upper eyelids, a rare birth defect known as *agenesis*, which causes painful irritation. Untreated, the condition probably would have led to ulceration and blindness. But using a groundbreaking procedure invented by Pavletic, Coster removed tissue from Phil's lip to reconstruct new eyelids. After the tissue was attached to the muscles above the eyes, little Phil was finally able to blink.

Coster was drawn to ophthalmology after rescuing from the streets his own cat, who had severe eye disease. "Watching his recovery and the return of his vision in the hands of skilled ophthalmologists is what opened my eyes to this specialty and the amazing things we can do. I also love the technology we get to employ to microscopically visualize the eye."

For his recent five-year "Angellversary," Coster calculated that he had performed almost nine thousand eye examinations and eight hundred surgeries. Nevertheless, he believes eye issues are often under-reported. "Our referring veterinarians do a fabulous job of referring eye cases to us, but I absolutely feel that a large percentage of cases do not ever make it to see a specialist. I think that there are so many people who come in expressing simple surprise that veterinary ophthalmologists even exist!"

Under the Skin: Dermatology

"There's a very low wow factor to what we do," admits Angell dermatologist Dr. Klaus Loft. "It's more heroic to be a surgeon or a cardiologist. But dermatology is like playing the game of Clue, because you can't ask the patient what's wrong and there's no single test to figure out what's happening. You have to rely on your diagnostic skills and work on symptoms and history to come up with some treatment, and you know when you're doing it right. It's very rewarding when you can see directly that you're making a difference."

With a caseload of roughly 2,500 appointments each year, Angell's Dermatology service is clearly making a difference. It's one of the two busiest dermatology departments in New England, and the only one that is part of a multi-specialty hospital, which can facilitate quick collaborations with other departments when needed. "I really enjoy that," Loft says. "You get to pick the brain or share your brain with other brilliant clinicians."

While Angell's Dermatology service occasionally sees skin cancers and autoimmune diseases, Loft says more than three-quarters of the department's caseload is allergy related. In fact, he estimates that more than 80 percent of all cats and dogs he sees have some kind of allergic disease. While they may not show it with frequent sneezing and watery eyes, dogs and cats are just as prone to allergies as people are, and Loft says skin and ear issues drive the majority of those seeking veterinary care. In addition to environmental causes, food allergies and flea allergy dermatitis can cause dogs and cats to scratch, chew, lick, and bite their paws, rub their face, or have recurrent ear infections.

"People may not perceive it as allergies," he explains, "but that's where we come in. A vet may treat a pet for years with chronic ear infections that could be a food allergy or something in the environment. Dogs can

Phil the cat in a playful moment post-surgery

be allergic to cats, to humans, to weed and grass pollen, to dust mites and other environmental allergens. But for them it manifests more as skin allergies, itchy skin rashes, hair loss, or chronic, reoccurring ear infections."

Loft says that allergies are something he addresses in all his appointments. "It's something you die with—not from—but the better you take care of them, the better the quality of life. A dog is not supposed to chew his feet or have an oily, scaly coat or frequent ear infections. It's important to educate clients about this. Dr. Google is not always their best friend."

Though most of the service's patients start out as referrals from outside Angell, many patients with chronic allergies are in for the long haul. "Since you can't cure allergies, you can only manage them, we have a lot of frequent fliers we get to be good friends with over many years," Loft says. "That's part of the fun—those client relationships."

Pet allergies have been a concern at Angell for decades, and in 2013, Angell became the first multi-specialty facility in New England to have a dedicated service with two full-time dermatologists on staff. Loft and fellow dermatology specialist Dr. Meghan Umstead are also developing the service's Ear Clinic as a separate entity, with sustainable caseloads and dedicated CT slots to diagnose and manage chronic ear infections in pets. They are working with Angell's Neurology department to obtain specialized equipment to use diagnostically for disease control and to aid in developing minimally invasive surgical techniques. Loft is developing special tools to facilitate techniques for some of the most delicate procedures. "Nobody else is doing that, and right now the tools we have need to be adjusted for each situation," he says.

Loft is dedicated to sharing his knowledge with other veterinarians, especially when it comes to innovative thinking. He recently returned from a veterinary dermatology conference where he presented one of his most interesting cases, a three-year-old Domestic Shorthair named Ozzy with a strange and rare disease called *feline idiopathic ulcerative dermatitis*. "It's a weird disease, not well described in the textbooks," Loft explains.

For eighteen months before Loft saw her, Ozzy had been continually scratching one spot on her neck until it was completely raw. It took almost two years to get the itchiness on the cat's neck under control, at one point using up to ten different medications a day to keep the poor cat comfortable.

"The owner is the only reason that cat's alive," Loft says. "She's one of my favorite clients. She would not give up, and we didn't either. It took a lot of effort and different approaches, and one lesion just wouldn't heal. We tried surgery and all these different techniques outside the norm. And we gave her ideas about some products to keep the cat from reaching the spot to scratch, and she developed a kind of donut collar, a sock with an inner foam ring that worked really well."

But it wasn't until Loft started thinking even more out of the box that he hit pay dirt. "I don't do well in the box," he confesses. "I like to keep coming up with solutions that don't follow all the rules. I know the rules and can be a good team player together with the rest of the crew—without them, I probably wouldn't be here." This rule-breaking solution involved a drug that was designed to treat the itch in humans and dogs but hadn't been tested for cats. It was a risk, but it proved to be wildly successful. Ozzy healed beautifully and is now doing really well on only that one medication.

"The owner sent me a very nice card around Christmas saying how grateful she was for all we had done for Ozzy," says Loft. And in the corner of the card, she included a little holiday message from the cat, who understandably never enjoyed his frequent forays to the vet: "And Ozzy says F U."

Loft laughs. "Best Christmas card ever."

Repair and Reconstruction: Surgery

Most animal owners, if they're lucky, never face the prospect of sending a beloved pet into major surgery once it is spayed. If they do, it's most commonly to remove a growth or something the animal ingested. "Young dogs and cats can get into a lot of mischief chewing on various objects," says Dr. Michael (Pav) Pavletic, Angell's Director of Surgery services. "If swallowed, they become foreign bodies that may cause serious problems, including intestinal obstruction leading to bowel perforation and physiologic derangements."

But for Angell surgeons, those common routines are just the tip of the iceberg. Today, the expertise of Angell surgeons embraces orthopedic, soft tissue, and trauma, and they perform a wide range of procedures, including fracture and ligament repair, neurosurgery, thoracic and abdominal surgery, laryngeal surgery, cancer surgery, and plastic and reconstructive surgery, often incorporating state-of-the-art arthroscopic and laparoscopic

Dr. Michael Pavletic,
Director of Surgery
services

procedures. Angell's surgical team can replace hips, lengthen limbs, or out-
fit them with prosthetics. They can repair a cleft palate, reconstruct a foot,
or remove a brain tumor. They can address trauma issues ranging from
bites and burns to gunshot wounds and injuries from being hit by vehicles.

The practice of surgery at Angell goes back to the hospital's very beginning in 1915, but it wasn't until 1965 that Angell established its own separate Department of Surgery under the guidance of Dr. C. Lawrence Blakely
and Dr. Robert Griffiths. Angell has been on the forefront of numerous
advancements in the understanding of best practices and the development
of innovative techniques. Early on, the use of an aseptic environment and
techniques became standard practice, radically reducing the possibility of
infection and cutting down the length of hospital stays. The development
and use of safer anesthesia gases made surgical procedures on older and
more frail patients less risky. Early Angell surgeons developed a number
of innovative procedures and techniques. Dr. Erwin F. Schroeder adapted
a human technique for repairing broken bones (the Schroeder-Thomas
Splint) that facilitated mobility while an injured fracture healed. Blakely

developed a groundbreaking repair for perineal hernias, and he and Dr. Todd Munson performed the first clinical case repair of a diaphragmatic hernia—using, of all things, a bicycle pump to ventilate the dog.

Over the decades, Angell surgical practices have become considerably more sophisticated, guided by a remarkable array of skilled, innovative surgeons, including the hospital's current team. Some of the most exciting work pioneered at Angell has been in reconstructive surgery, and groundbreaking procedures innovated by Pavletic have put the hospital on the forefront of the field.

When he first arrived at Angell as an intern in 1974, Pavletic was frequently confronted in the ER with wounds so severe that euthanasia seemed the only humane choice. But when he encountered a sweet old cat named John Glenn who had a large, seemingly inoperable facial tumor, Pavletic thought there must be some way he could help the poor animal. Instead of giving up, he began looking for answers outside the confines of veterinary medicine. "I realized that there was very little written on plastic or reconstructive surgery, and that stimulated me to study and try to learn more and more."

In the Angell library, he found an old human medicine reconstructive surgery book that was destined to be thrown out and began searching through it for ideas. Sparked by one of the reconstruction flap techniques he found in the book, he adapted a similar procedure for the cat, pioneering a new approach to veterinary medicine that has since saved countless lives and inspired veterinary surgeons around the world.

A leading authority on plastic and reconstructive surgery for small animals, Pavletic has pioneered more than seventy different techniques, ranging from facial and nasal reconstructive surgery down to reconstruction of the foot after trauma or tumor removal. He also developed several muscle flap techniques for closing massive chest and abdominal wall defects after trauma and wide resection of neoplasms. Over the past several years, Dr. Pavletic has adapted techniques to restore the pinna (visible part of the ear) of dogs and cats after tumor removal, rather than amputating the ear. In fact, most of the advanced skin flap techniques used today in veterinary surgery were developed by Dr. Pavletic. His innovations have extended to wound management, urinary tract reconstructive surgery, and surgical stapling techniques for thoracic and gastrointestinal surgery.

He has written for more than one hundred publications, sharing Angell's advancements with veterinarians around the world. When a mixed-breed Terrier named Sugar Plum came in after ingesting lye, Pavletic reconstructed the dog's cervical esophagus using skin from his neck. "The usual two options would have been to humanely euthanize him or form a permanent opening in his stomach and tube feed," he says. "But part of the joy of a dog's life is eating, and to deny that part of his life was not in the best interest of the dog. So presented with the situation, I asked myself, *How can I fix this?*"

He knew the skin tube technique had been used in humans in the past, so he applied the concept to creating a new esophagus for the dog. "It's a technique that still works, and I do consultations with vets throughout the world, helping them do the same thing," he says.

When a Border Collie named Bella injured her leg in a fall, causing her triceps muscle to contract and freeze in place, Pavletic came up with a new technique to transfer the latissimus dorsi muscle from the adjacent chest wall that could be "trained" to do the work of the original muscle. "Every week that goes by there's a different kind of challenge at Angell that requires some form of plastic surgery," he says.

With modern advances, veterinary surgical care has edged ever closer to the capabilities of human medicine. "Most new technological breakthroughs occur initially in human surgery, and many are adapted to veterinary surgery over time," says Pavletic. He should know. The memory of John Glenn the cat and the old reconstructive surgery book inspires him still.

Heroic Measures: Rufus' Story

For fifteen minutes, Rufus Dreeszen Bowman was technically dead. The scruffy eight-year-old Cocker Spaniel mix had come into Angell for a total ear canal ablation, a surgery considered a last resort to deal with chronic painful ear infections. But toward the end of the operation, the unexpected happened—Rufus went into cardiac arrest. Fortunately, Angell vets are well prepared for the unexpected.

Responding to the call for a code in the Emergency Room, Dr. Virginia Sinnott and resident Dr. Annie Wayne found that the surgeons had already started chest compressions, and the anesthesia technician had given two common medicines used to restart the heart (epinephrine and atropine). However, Rufus still had no pulse. The two emergency doctors took over and gave a newer CPR medication (vasopressin), which is often helpful when an animal has been in arrest for a longer period of time. At that point, Rufus' ECG went from flat-line to fibrillation, when the heart contracts rapidly and irregularly. Sinnott recalls, "We shocked him once, and the fine fibrillation became coarse, but at this point he'd been 'dead' for fifteen minutes. We were thinking of stopping the code, when he seemed to move his paw. His surgeon, Dr. Megan Sullivan, tearfully asked us to try again. We shocked him again, and *got him back!*"

Against all odds, Rufus' heart returned to a normal rhythm. However, the doctors were concerned about trauma to the dog's brain during his arrest and how that would impact his neurologic function. In a coma and not breathing well on his own, Rufus was moved to the Critical Care Unit, where he was stitched up and placed on a ventilator. For the next three hours, the ventilator kept Rufus alive, breathing for him. Dr. Sinnott remembers, "Usually when we ventilate dogs, we need upwards of four different sedatives to keep them asleep. Rufus needed *no* drugs because his brain had suffered such a great injury, and we weren't sure if the dog that the owners knew would ever come back to them."

Then Rufus slowly began to wake up, moving his paws and jaw, fighting the ventilation tube. He was allowed to come off the ventilator and breathe on his own while the doctors carefully monitored his oxygen and blood electrolytes, especially his high potassium level. (Though potassium is a necessary mineral, when the level in the blood is very high, it can be toxic to the heart.) Over the next twelve hours, Rufus was given IV fluids and medications, and slowly his potassium level came back to normal.

As his body began to heal, Rufus received pain medicine for the bruising caused during CPR and was started on precautionary medication for a one-time seizure that likely had been caused by the brain injury from the arrest. But he went home four days later and, according to his owner, is the same old Rufus she's always known and loved—with one exception. Before the surgery, Rufus was a bit nippy and cranky with strangers. He has since mellowed and has more energy, probably because the pain of his chronic ear infections is now gone. He is still just as mischievous, however. Not long after his surgery, he was back at Angell after he snatched some dark chocolate that had accidentally been left in his reach. Sinnott recalls, "He'd been groomed and no longer had bad ear infections, so I barely recognized him. He was sweet and spirited—and very hyper—probably from all that chocolate!" While often Angell veterinarians are challenged with thinking out of the box to solve a new problem, at other times it is more a matter of simply not giving up.

The True Insiders: Primary Care and Internal Medicine

As a full-service veterinary hospital, a big part of Angell's activity is dedicated to Primary Care/Wellness services. Angell maintains a large team of veterinarians and support staff dedicated to the kinds of primary care animals need on a regular, ongoing basis, such as annual exams, vaccinations, and flea/tick prevention. Nutrition expertise plays into care as well, not just for healthy pets and geriatric needs, but for the unique metabolic requirements of patients with a wide variety of medical conditions.

Most of the veterinarians have additional specialty interests, from dermatology and endocrinology to geriatrics, and their expertise and insight are well suited for most common pet issues. Cultivating long-term care, they are the doctors who know their patients best.

However, sometimes an animal comes in with a more complicated problem or symptoms that don't have an obvious cause. Maybe a dog is unusually lethargic or a cat is off her food, and routine diagnostics aren't providing a ready answer. Many vets use the "highly technical" term ADR— as in "ain't doin' right"—and sometimes time proves to be the best cure. However, if conventional wisdom and common measures aren't able to resolve an issue, the next step is often to consult with another doctor.

Veterinarians who see internal medicine cases tend not to like the ADR designation. Dr. Douglas Brum explains, "I kind of want to get to the bottom of why an animal is not doing right. I want to take the next step."

Internal medicine is the backbone of Angell's non-emergency practice. Angell's team has decades of experience as well as expertise in a range of medical specialties to complement the skill set of the primary care veterinarian. After years of advanced training and a rigorous certification process, the internist can look at the complete picture of a pet's current issues in light of its health history, piecing together clinical signs, lab results, imaging studies, and special testing, then filtering that information through a knowledge of immune disorders, infectious diseases, and the internal systems of the body. Internists treat a wide range of diseases affecting the kidneys, liver, gastrointestinal tract, endocrine glands, lungs, and bone marrow. They also routinely perform a number of specialized procedures that aid in more refined diagnostics as well as treatment, from ultrasounds and aspirations to biopsies and foreign body retrieval (for example, removing that tiny toy the dog ate).

A Day in the Life: Internal Medicine Veterinarian Dr. Douglas Brum

There are many beloved and influential veterinarians at Angell; Dr. Douglas Brum, an Angell fixture since 1987, is just one of them. His office on the first floor of the old building frequently accommodates one of his giant dogs (a Bernese Mountain Dog and a Leonberger) stretched full length on the floor like a furry rug. He has a wide practice of long-time clients and also sees many internal medicine cases.

Brum has been known to forgo rounds to squeeze in longtime patients who have become acutely ill. He checks in constantly with Maureen Sweeney, the indispensable veterinary technician who keeps him on track during the day, and the intern rotating through the program's "Brum-tern," a chance to work intensively with Brum for three to five dedicated weeks. Mentoring the interns, whom Brum calls "the heart and soul of the hospital," is one of his passions, and he was able to get the "Brum-tern" endowed through business contributions by two grateful clients.

"I'm so lucky I get to have them one-on-one," he maintains. "They're so special, really smart. They keep you young, interested. They have all these great ideas. Interns help me every day to find out current thinking on a disease. They'll spend an hour researching on the web or call another professor to find out information. And I really need the extra help of an intern to be able to do all that I do. They can see referrals, and it allows us to work as a team."

This week, Amanda Rollins has the privilege of the Brum-tern. As she, Brum, and Sweeney discuss ongoing cases and the day's schedule, planning who may need X-rays, ultrasounds, and blood work, his assistant, Jen McManus, checks in by phone. She's worked with Brum roughly twenty-five years as the intermediary between the doctor, his patients, and the numerous vets who refer cases to him, conveying information and facilitating appointments.

Brum's first scheduled appointment of the day is a checkup of a long-standing patient with a variety of non-life-threatening issues, a ten-year-old yellow Lab named Heather. Brum strides through the lobby and waves the dog and her owner over to the weigh-in station. "Hey, Maynard," he says jovially, greeting Paul Maynard, the dog's owner. "Come on over, Heather, you know the routine."

In the examining room, Brum warms up the nervous dog with a cookie. "Sit," he says firmly. Heather complies and scarfs down the cookie as Brum turns to Maynard. "What's going on? Got a list for me?" They go through the half-dozen medications that have stabilized Heather's kidney issues over the years, and Brum gives the dog a thorough once over. "Whenever a pet comes in, we do a full exam," he explains.

Brum is down on the floor, Sweeney trying to distract the dog with treats, when the vet's brow wrinkles with a slight grimace of concentration. He has found something totally unexpected, a mass in Heather's anal sac. "I think we have a problem," he tells the concerned owner. "I'm hoping it's an infection, but it could also be a tumor, and that's a bad spot for it." They decide to get a sample, and Sweeney takes Heather into the clinic area. What was supposed to be fairly routine has suddenly become much more complex—and time-consuming.

Brum takes the dog back into the exam room. He says, "Let's get Kathy on the phone." Kathy, Maynard's wife, works in retail and as a dog walker, so he is the one who brings Heather to most appointments. Kathy has a very emotional attachment to the dog, and Brum knows he needs to fill her in personally with what's going on. He details what he's found so far and what the possible next steps might be. She is clearly distraught. He is soothing and reassuring, but medically straightforward. He tells her, "Let me run the sample down to the lab to see what we have, and I'll call you back."

And he does just that, sprinting down the hall and down the stairs to Angell's pathology office. Rollins walks alongside, her computer open, filling Brum in on his next patient, a thirteen-year-old cat, referred by another vet, with abdominal fluid and a history of thyroid issues. The cat and her owners have come all the way from Nantucket.

Dr. Douglas Brum, Internal Medicine

Pathologist Patty Ewing immediately checks Brum's slide under the microscope, and within seconds she has an answer—it's not an infection, it's a tumor. "This is bad, so upsetting," Brum says, but the quick turn-around (unheard of in human hospitals, he claims) will let him give Heather's owners information right away. Angell is one of the only veterinary hospitals in the Northeast with in-house pathology services. Brum stops by the ultrasound room on the way, requesting they squeeze in Heather as an overbook so he can see if the tumor has spread. "Thanks. You guys rock!" he says with a wave.

"I like what I do," he says, "and I like the people I work with. These people work so hard and have the best interests of the animals at heart and really want to do a good job. And it's always been like that." He recalls during his early years on staff one particularly busy day removing stitches and tubes from a cat in the waiting room because all the exam rooms were full, likening his job to working in a M.A.S.H. unit. But he grew deeply attached to the place then, and nearly three decades on, he is still the hospital's reigning "can do" spirit.

At 10:15, Brum checks with Rollins, who has already seen the cat, about her findings and the test results from the cat's previous vet. Then he goes into the exam room to chat with the owners. Everyone is quickly put at ease, and the sweet gray cat lets Brum examine her swollen belly. He explains the three possible sources of the fluid. "I'd like to start in steps," he suggests, and they agree on an abdominal ultrasound and draining some of the fluid to get a sample for analysis and to relieve some of the cat's discomfort. Rollins takes the cat to the clinic, and Brum moves on to the next patient.

Later, while Brum is catching up on paperwork, Rollins zips by with information on another referral she has been managing, an eleven-year-old German Shorthaired Pointer named Oliver with increased drinking and peeing, often a red flag. The dog recently had his spleen removed, but he is still having issues. He is very skinny, Rollins tells Brum. Could it be Cushing's, they speculate? "What's weird about this?" Brum asks her, Socratic fashion.

She thinks a moment. "You'd expect him to be overweight," she says, and he nods.

He asks, "So what do we want to do?"

Rollins suggests repeating blood work and a chest X-ray, and Brum suggests aspirating the lymph node as well. "So when we go in the room now, we have a plan."

Oliver is pacing and pawing at the door, but when Brum squats down to examine him, he gives the doctor a brisk welcome lick in the face. Brum gently pokes and palpates the dog, asking about allergies and other physical symptoms. He outlines possible diagnoses, including those from psychogenic causes, before sending Oliver off for tests.

It's 11:00 by the time Brum gets back to Heather and Maynard, who have been waiting patiently. With the slides showing a tumor, Maynard gets his wife on the phone again to discuss a possible surgery and the potential for malignancy. Her pain and fear come through the phone's speaker as she tries to choke back tears, but Brum deftly calms her down. He wants to have Dr. Mike Pavletic examine Heather and do the surgery as soon as possible. "It could be benign, but if it's malignant, we'll talk about options," he reassures her. "We could still give her some good time. I'll have a better idea once I talk to the surgeon and get more test results today. Hang in."

Rollins brings Oliver's X-rays by. Brum examines them, finds nothing of real interest, and clears the dog for release. Results of blood work will be phoned in. It's after noon, so he walks into an exam room to find a phone to check in with Jen, scanning e-mails on his smartphone. "I see I have ninety-two unread e-mails," he remarks wryly.

It's 12:40, and Brum has two more patients to squeeze in before rounds at 1:00—that's when interns present the details of the cases under their care and get feedback from doctors and residents. "We examine each animal, check medication dosages. It's a good learning experience for everybody, a kind of checks and balances to make sure everyone's on the right track."

After rounds, there are more appointments, including a dog that ate a shoe and most probably will need surgery to remove leather bits obstructing his small intestine. And there are dozens of e-mails to address and calls to return . . .

Once again, Brum's out the door, Sweeney hurrying behind to catch up.

Comfort for All: Client Services

One of the key ingredients of Angell's remarkable success is the hospital's ability to respond not only to the needs of animals, but to those, as President Carter Luke puts it, "at the other end of the lead." Most people nowadays would not hesitate to call their pets family members, and when any family members are injured or ill, all the loved ones involved bear a considerable burden of stress. Part of Angell's stability and its solidity during the nation's economic downturn, which weakened many businesses and nonprofits, is due to its leadership under Dr. Ann Marie Greenleaf, who focused her staff on the human side of veterinary care. Angell had always been the best at taking care of animals; under Greenleaf it would recognize the needs of those animals' faithful caregivers.

Under this new focus, staff members were retrained in all client services, and in 2012, Angell launched one of its most revolutionary initiatives, the Client Care Coordinators program. Dedicated to an intensive level of customer care and service, it has transformed the way the hospital relates not just to the pets admitted for procedures or monitoring, but also to the families waiting anxiously. While the doctors and technicians tend to their patients, the Client Care Coordinators attend to the needs of their worried owners, providing up-to-the-minute information on their pets' welfare.

"This is a very unusual program," says Mary Grace, Angell's Director of Hospital Operations. "We have nine care coordinators dedicated to caring for the clients, not the pets. When an animal is admitted, a coordinator talks to the client about what the process will be. They take information about how and when families would like communication about how their pet is doing; then they hover around the treatment areas to seek out information from the doctors so they can provide updates. They can say 'Your dog is settled in . . . just went into surgery . . . just woke up . . .' They can text or e-mail goodnight and good-morning photos. It's very personal. They are the point people every step of the way about how the pet is doing until the doctor can call and provide the clinical details. I've had vice presidents of human hospitals saying they wish that they had this kind of program for their clients. It's all about setting appropriate expectations and then exceeding them."

Any time a pet comes into the hospital for more than routine care, Client Care Coordinators are involved from the beginning and stay involved until discharge and often beyond, serving as a direct conduit between the client and the doctor. It's an intensive job with an impressive amount of responsibility, and all coordinators have at least two years prior veterinary practice experience. Coordinators meet clients at check-in and take charge of drop-off patients, moving the animal through the clinic, making introductions to ward staff, and double-checking paperwork. At discharge, coordinators can schedule pick-up time and recheck appointments, arrange for any prescriptions, and talk to clients about medications and care at home. They also continue the connection while the patient recovers at home and on subsequent visits.

However, the primary charge is to relay messages between doctors and clients while a patient is in the hospital to keep the client informed and reassured. "Clients come in with their pets for a procedure and they're an absolute nervous wreck," says Client Care Coordinator Jeanne David-Lee. "Their pets are like their children. My job is to reassure them, to tell them

I'll sit with their pet and calm it down if it's nervous, send them pictures to reassure them, call as soon as their pet is under anesthesia. People say they feel so much better knowing their pet is not just stuck in a cage. There's a lot of satisfaction in helping clients breathe a little easier while their pet is here."

David-Lee says the most challenging part of her job is when a situation involves a terminal diagnosis. "Sometimes a pet comes in with seizures, they do an MRI and find a brain tumor, and there's nothing they can do. When you have to discharge that animal, it's hard seeing the look on clients' faces, knowing their pets are just going home to live out the best quality of life for as long as they can."

Psychological insight and sensitivity are a huge part of the job. David-Lee takes that a step further. She says she gives clients her phone and e-mail information if they ask, and they sometimes reach out to her weeks or months after their pets have gone home. Often it's to ask for help in deciding about euthanasia. "They contact me and describe symptoms, ask 'Does this sound like the end? Do you it's think time to let go now?' I want to reassure them as best I can, tell them that their pet knows it is loved and that they are doing their best and that they'll know when it's time. I'm always here for them. I check e-mails from home and even answer at night, if I think it's something that someone is really stressing over."

And if a patient comes in and its owner and the doctor agree that euthanasia is the appropriate option, David-Lee says the Client Care Coordinators can help facilitate that process as well. "We have a beautiful private room, and we take families in and explain what's going to happen. We bring the pet to the room and let them have as much time alone as they need together. When they say they're ready, the doctor will go in and start an IV, and stay with the family until they make sure the pet is gone. I always say, 'I'm right outside the door if you need me.' When clients ask me to be with them, I feel very honored. That means I've been doing my job right in making it easier for them. And a lot of times, I hug and comfort them and cry right along, I'm that touched." Sometimes owners ask the coordinators to make a paw print of their animal in clay or cut a tuft of fur in remembrance.

Like most of the Client Care Coordinators, David-Lee has a trove of thank-you notes that attest to the difference their services have made. And though client care is the coordinators' mission, sometimes caring for the client means extra attention for the pet as well. One of David-Lee's most memorable experiences involved a sweet-natured four-year-old Doberman Pinscher named Sigmund (Siggy), who needed eighteen radiation treatments in the summer of 2014 for a tumor. Normally, the patient would be brought in every day for two and a half weeks. However, Siggy's owners, Jim and Margie Kerouac, lived more than two hours away in New Hampshire, so the plan was to board the dog Monday through Friday for three weeks.

When David-Lee first met the couple, they were waiting to drop Siggy off for his first treatment, and Margie was in tears. David-Lee recalls, "I went over and said, 'Can I pet your Doberman? I have a Doberman, too.' She said, 'Then you understand what big babies they are.' She was so worried about leaving him overnight, and she really got to me. I told her that I would personally watch over Siggy while he was here."

That reassurance seemed to calm the couple, but Siggy had trouble with the separation. After they left, he seemed so stressed out that David-Lee called them and asked if she could take Siggy to her office with her during the day. That seemed to make all the difference. David-Lee says, "He did great with that. I joke that I put him to work answering the phones." For three weeks, David-Lee basically babysat the dog, bonding with him and sending his owners frequent pictures and videos, including shots of Siggy manning her desk.

"We truly appreciated how much she cared for Sigmund," Jim Kerouac says. "She not only brought him to her office, she held him while they sedated him, played ball with him, posted pictures of him to the Angell Facebook page. And on his last day, which was also his birthday, she baked him a cake and gave him a personalized bag with toys and treats to celebrate."

The Kerouacs come back to Angell every few months for Siggy's follow-up appointments, and David-Lee says Margie always tells her she couldn't have left Siggy if it hadn't been for her. Margie says, "Siggy *loves* Jeanne. She is a very caring and positive person. We can't thank her enough for putting us at ease at all times during Siggy's treatment. We always knew that he was in good hands and that he was getting the care, love, and attention that we

Siggy manning the phone

would want any family member to receive when going through such an intensive treatment. Having Jeanne as Sigmund's Patient Care Coordinator made a difficult and scary time much easier on us and on Siggy."

David-Lee says, "It really makes a difference to have a Client Care Coordinator. It's amazing to me that human hospitals don't provide this service."

Helping with the Cost: Financial Assistance

Client Care Coordinators can also help pet owners better understand hospital processes and policies, including the financial considerations, such as cost estimates, deposit requirements, and payment methods. As research and technology have facilitated more sophisticated diagnostic testing and treatment procedures, veterinary care has become more expensive, and pet insurance is still relatively uncommon. While Angell's state-of-the-art systems allow doctors to pursue the most complete picture of an animal's health and treat accordingly, they try to be mindful that not all families have the resources for exhaustive testing and procedures. Virtually every staff member at Angell has at least one heartbreak story about the pet whose owner couldn't afford the cost of further diagnostics or treatment.

"We work hard to get services to an affordable amount, but the kind of specialty care we offer is expensive," admits Mary Grace, Angell's Director of Hospital Operations. "Treating a cat who has eaten a piece of string can cost two thousand dollars. It's painful to sit across from someone and want to help their pet, but they can't afford the cost, and we can't subsidize everyone."

Families with sick pets are often faced with tough choices, but staff members are trained to connect clients who are eligible with Angell's Financial Assistance program. Angell has a long history of taking care of animals whose owners could not cover the cost of treatment. As a non-profit charitable organization, the MSPCA–Angell provides medical care for abused animals and homeless animals, as well as animals whose owners need financial assistance in order to meet their animals' medical needs. In 2014, for example, the MSPCA–Angell spent $2,153,221 on those animals needing special support.

But over the past half-decade, not only low-income families but also middle-class pet owners who've lost their jobs often have been finding themselves in need. Angell has three programs, all funded by donations that help defray the cost of treatment: Pet Care Assistance, the Additional Care Fund, and Senior Assistance. The Pet Care Assistance program at the MSPCA–Angell was established in 1990 to provide funds for three basic purposes: to support medical care at Angell Animal Medical Center for sick or injured animals whose owners have limited financial resources, to support the medical care of abused or neglected animals connected with their Law Enforcement efforts, and to support the medical care of homeless animals in their adoption centers. Grace says many people are drawn to Angell because they know financial help is available.

And sometimes help comes from unexpected places. Grace says, "We have doctors and staff, even hourly employees, who have contributed out of pocket in certain cases. It makes such a big difference to get a pet well enough to walk out the door."

Rescuing the Rescued

Having the MSPCA Law Enforcement officers and adoption center staff all quartered in the same building as the Angell medical personnel is a huge boon for animals in trouble. Angell veterinarians are frequently called upon to consult on or treat dogs, cats, and other creatures who, for whatever reason, have ended up in one of the MSPCA's adoption centers. Injuries or illnesses too grave to be cared for in the adoption center treatment rooms can be transferred to the staff at Angell for ongoing treatment until they are well enough to be adopted out. Some of these animals come to the MSPCA through Law Enforcement seizures or surrenders. Some are hoarding cases; some are cases of outright neglect or cruelty. But one thing they all have in common is that no one knows when they'll burst through Angell's doors. The staff at Angell is always prepared.

One such case came to Angell in June 2011, on a day when the news was dominated by a massive heat wave that broiled living things all across the country. Caring pet owners took special precautions so their animals wouldn't become overheated, and made sure their pets' bowls were kept full of fresh water.

But in Tewksbury, Massachusetts, thirteen Pointers, one Labrador Retriever, and three cats were locked up together in a dark blue van sitting in a boiling-hot parking lot while their owner napped inside an air-conditioned motel. All the windows in the van were closed.

The temperature inside that van was estimated to be well over one hundred degrees, and the animals had been imprisoned there for more than five hours. By the time the Tewksbury Police and MSPCA Law Enforcement were alerted, one of the dogs had already died, and many of the others were severely dehydrated and weak. The animals' owner was immediately placed under arrest and charged with animal cruelty.

The cats and eleven of the dogs, most of them extremely thin, were transported to the MSPCA's nearby facility at Nevins Farm, but two of the dogs required more intensive medical treatment and were taken to Angell Animal Medical Center in Boston. After being treated for their various urgent problems, including serious skin and eye infections, the animals were spayed or neutered in preparation for finding them new homes. Angell absorbed the full cost of their care. The collaborative nature of this undertaking is a common occurrence at the MSPCA–Angell, where it's all about the animals, 24 hours a day, 365 days a year.

These dogs and cats did eventually find new homes, The new family of one of the Pointers, now named Jet, noted that the dog had some adjustment problems at first, but he soon began doing really well and is loving his new life—and all the people who love him back.

From Strays to Stars

Like any large urban hospital, Angell's clientele over the decades has ranged from strays, runaways, foundlings, and a host of abused animals rescued by the MSPCA to police and fire department service dogs to the most pampered of pets, including Elvis Presley's ailing Chow Chow, whom the King flew in from Memphis to be cared for at Angell. Shortly after the hospital moved from the Longwood Avenue site into the facility in Jamaica Plain, one family drove up from the Cape, looking for a veterinarian to help their beloved Alpine goat, Jewel, give birth. Angell's Dr. Charles Patterson performed a caesarian section on the animal, bringing two adorable kids into the world.

Pet owners with little money but abundant love for their animals bring their charges to Angell by foot or public transportation. Others, drawn by

Jet, a rescued Pointer, running on the beach

the hospital's international reputation, have arrived in stretch limos and Rolls-Royces. They have flown in from overseas on the Concorde or on military jets. In fact, shortly after the hospital moved from the Longwood Avenue site into the facility in Jamaica Plain, one little pug that was experiencing a bout of intestinal inflammation was flown in from Switzerland. He was treated, and two days later he and his owner jetted back to Europe.

Numerous four-legged television stars such as Lassie and the Lone Ranger's beloved horse, Silver, have been treated by Angell staff, as have, considerably more recently, the dogs of Patriots quarterback Tom Brady and Gisele Bündchen. Stephen King brought his Welsh Corgi Marlowe down to Angell from Bangor, Maine, and John Kerry's dog has been a regular Angell patient. Staffers recall when the Secretary of State himself brought the dog to Angell with the Secret Service in tow, their dark SUVs idling in the parking lot.

Current Chief of Staff Ann Marie Greenleaf

CHAPTER 9

Regroup and Reaffirm

AT ITS LARGEST, the MSPCA–Angell had a network of three Angell Animal Medical Centers—in Boston, Western New England (Springfield), and Nantucket. But when the financial crisis of 2008 caused the country's most severe recession since World War II, the MSPCA–Angell felt the hit. Economic strains forced significant reductions to staff throughout the organization. The animal welfare programs Living with Wildlife and Phinney's Friends were reluctantly eliminated.

In 2009, the MSPCA sold its Springfield facility, which included an animal hospital and adoption center, to Dakin Pioneer Valley Humane Society (DPVHS) for a discounted price, enabling DPVHS to expand its successful programs from Hampshire and Franklin counties to Hampden county. On Martha's Vineyard, Nantucket, and in Brockton, the MSPCA facilities were turned over to local entities. The MSPCA–Martha's Vineyard Animal Care and Adoption Center officially became the Animal Shelter of Martha's Vineyard (ASMV) in 2009. The MSPCA Metro South Animal Care and Adoption Center in Brockton also closed that year, and a new nonprofit, the Animal Protection Center of Southeastern Massachusetts, was formed to continue to serve the animals and people in the Brockton area. In 2011, four top Nantucket veterinarians purchased the MSPCA facility on Nantucket, satisfying the MSPCA–Angell's goal to find a buyer committed to providing the community with high-quality veterinary hospital care on the island.

Angell began to get back on its feet, largely through the efforts of Dr. Ann Marie Greenleaf (formerly Ann Marie Manning), who became Chief of Staff at Angell Animal Medical Center. She received her degree in veterinary medicine from the Tufts University School of Veterinary Medicine in 1993 and became a diplomate of the American College of Emergency and

Critical Care Medicine in 1997. Dr. Greenleaf began her career at Angell in 1997 as an emergency and critical care veterinarian and was promoted first to Chief Medical Officer in 2004, and then to Chief of Staff in 2008. President Carter Luke announced her promotion in an e-mail to Angell staff by saying, "Here's a test concerning some MSPCA–Angell history: What do these four people have in common? Gerry Schnelle, Gus Thornton, Paul Gambardella, Ann Marie Manning? . . . Yes, they were/are all veterinarians . . . yes, they were/are some of the finest doctors in the world at the finest veterinary hospital in the world. . . . Yes, they were/are medical leaders of Angell . . . going back to 1950. . . . Dr. Ann Marie Manning certainly deserves to be mentioned in the same breath as those others. . . . They were all called Chief of Staff. And effective immediately, that's Ann Marie's title as well."

Dr. Ann Marie Greenleaf

Dr. Greenleaf directs the entire Angell staff and oversees all hospital programs, working closely with hospital staff, department directors, and the referring veterinary community to ensure that the highest standards of quality and service are maintained. Dr. Greenleaf oversees the implementation of quality improvement efforts designed to maximize clinical performance and maintain compliance with the American Animal Hospital Association.

Under Dr. Greenleaf's direction, the hospital undertook a dramatic $4 million turnaround. She committed to giving excellent communication to referring partners and improving efficiency in processes throughout the hospital. She worked to revamp how the hospital awarded financial assistance so that more people could be helped, and she started the Client Care Coordinator program to give clients an experience that matched the quality of Angell's medicine and surgery.

With Dr. Greenleaf's help, Angell continues to look at ways to improve the patient experience—simple things like decreasing squeaky wheels on gurneys, shutting off lights in the wards at night, and providing warm blankets for cats on exam tables. She is dedicated to improving the big picture as well as the details.

"Our goal," Dr. Greenleaf says, "is to continue to change and evolve so that we get better and better and do not settle for status quo or just doing a good job. We try to do a *great* job. We listen to all feedback from clients and referring veterinarians so we can meet their needs and aid our evolution. I suppose there are people who say that we are more businesslike, but I believe we had to think more about our client and market like any business does to make sure we stay relevant and deliver the best services we can."

In 2012, the hospital initiated leadership training for the management team at Angell. Major and minor renovations have been completed, and staff is strategically hired to meet market demands.

Dedicated animal lovers all, Dr. Greenleaf's own family shares their home with sixteen chickens (six adopted from the MSPCA), and three cats and two dogs (all adopted from the MSPCA). Their seventeen-year-old cat was one of the first patients Dr. Greenleaf ever treated at Angell.

Continual Evolution

Angell is dedicated to continual improvement. In the MSPCA's 2013 annual report, Luke summed up a new approach for the entire organization. He wrote,

> Compassion. Integrity. Positivity. Service. Excellence. Collaboration. These aren't just words; they are the core values that motivate us to work hard every day for the animals in our care. A cross-section of MSPCA–Angell employees, representing every function under our roof, came together in 2013 to outline and initiate a historic cultural shift to a consciously values-based organization. The result is the documentation of a set of values that has always been embedded in the fabric of our organization, and which will now be carefully applied to everything we do, from hands-on animal care to performance evaluations and new-hire criteria. We are living our values. We all felt strongly that "compassion" should top the list, for not only is it a beautiful word that echoes throughout every single thing we do here, but it appears in our mission statement, where we affirm that we are striving "for a just and compassionate society."

Angell Animal Medical Center in the twenty-first century has evolved into a medical mecca as well as one of the world's foremost veterinary teaching hospitals. It is also one of an elite group of hospitals representing only 12 to 15 percent of all small animal practices to receive accreditation from the American Animal Hospital Association following comprehensive evaluations of the hospital's facility, medical equipment, practice methods, and pet health-care management to meet over nine hundred standards.

In 2014, Angell's staff included 73 veterinarians, and the caseload was over 61,000, with more than 16,000 new patients. More than 16,500 patients received emergency care, and over 13,000 surgeries were performed. In addition, MSPCA–Angell West opened in February 2014, providing 24-7 emergency care as well as a number of specialty services, including Internal Medicine, Surgery, Avian/Exotic, and Cardiology. During the first ten months the facility was open, the caseload there was more than 4,500, including more than 1,100 new patients.

CODA

Looking Toward the Future

George Thorndike Angell's legacy lives on in the countless animals and animal lovers touched by the work of the remarkable medical center named in his honor. As Angell Animal Medical Center looks toward its next one hundred years, the hospital is poised to maintain its role as a leading center of compassionate veterinary care. At the time of this book's publication, Angell is in the midst of its second capital campaign, a $25 million effort that will enable the hospital's innovative work to continue. This successful campaign will provide Angell caregivers with up-to-date equipment and renovated space, and it will allow more animals to receive top-of-the-line treatment by offering financial aid to economically strained owners. Angell's next century of excellence continues to depend on the generosity of people who can replenish this priceless resource through their contributions. With their help, Angell Animal Medical Center will always remain a dynamic, passionate family of diagnosticians and healers, all working collaboratively to make animals well.